The Lafayette Collection

———— ❧ ————

Cover art by Lynda Dann Keally
From the collection of Linda and Terry Murray

Design by Henry Simpson

Benefitting The Lafayette School District
1991

The Lafayette School District, located in Lafayette, California, is comprised of four elementary schools: Burton Valley, Happy Valley, Lafayette School, and Springhill; as well as the Stanley Intermediate School. Serving nearly 3,000 students, with a strong commitment to excellence, Lafayette consistently ranks among the top school districts in the State of California.

All proceeds realized from the sale of *The Lafayette Collection* will directly benefit the students of the Lafayette School District.

To order additional copies of *The Lafayette Collection* contact:

> *The Lafayette Collection*
> c/o The Lafayette School District
> P. O. Box 1029
> Lafayette, CA 94549
> Telephone: 510/284-7011

Acknowledgments

*T*he *Lafayette Collection* has become a reality as a result of literally hundreds of people donating thousands of hours and dollars. The foundation for the cookbook's success is built of over 1,500 recipes, 177 testing families, 6,000 recipe evaluations, 198 page sponsors and 425 honor roll sponsors. The process has been a partnership in the truest sense of the word. The support of the parents clubs and PTA's; of the Lafayette business community, of the principals, teachers and staffs of the schools; of the school board, the district office and of countless families and friends has happened to an extent far greater and in ways far more diverse than could ever have been imagined.

For her advice, support and encouragement we are very grateful to:

Marion Cunningham

For their significant individual contributions special thanks to:

Sharon Bliss
Steve Brooks
Connie Collier
J. Alan Constant
Barbara Flores
Leon Kolinski
Eleanor Lindheimer
Barclay and Sharon Simpson
Elyse Sottero
George Sottero

Note from the Committee

Our singular purpose in producing this cookbook has been to enhance the education of Lafayette children. A second benefit has been the development of a cooperative community spirit.

Eighteen months ago, it was decided that a cookbook would be created and sold. The funds generated from this project would be used to ensure that the quality programs jeopardized by budget constraints would continue. It has taken our time, our creativity, our patience and our good humor but it will always be a fond memory for us all.

With thanks and congratulations to our community who made it happen and our very special gratitude to Dick, Keith, Ken, Neil and Terry, we dedicate this book to the kids we all love so much.

The Cookbook Committee

Marcia Thomas
Chairman

Diane Kelly
Burton Valley School

Chris Cameron
Happy Valley School

Linda Murray
Lafayette School

Linda Staaf
Springhill School

*T*he *Lafayette Collection* is the result of hundreds of volunteers generously contributing thousands of hours of their time.

For more than 7 months, as each of the over 1,500 recipes was submitted, food editors at each of the 4 schools met weekly to review and clarify the recipes prior to testing. During the 4 month testing period, they were on call to answer the many questions from the testing families. When the testing process was finished, the food editors reviewed the evaluations, retested the recipes, rewrote the directions and made the initial selection of the recipes that appear in the book. For their dedication, enthusiasm and talent we are grateful to the following food editors:

Kathy Babcock

Kim Brast

Jean Brillant

Martha Harris

Cashie Kieckhefer

Karen Maggio

Recipe librarians at each of the 4 schools received each recipe as it was submitted, recorded it, distributed it to 4 individual testing families, and collected the testers' written evaluations. For their tremendous contribution to the cookbook, we thank the following recipe librarians:

Kim Brast

Jean Brillant

Judy Boriskin

Judy Garden

Linda Ulbrich

*F*or testing and retesting all of the recipes, our thanks to the families of:

Chris Anders	Sharon Cooley	Kathy Gilmour
Karen Anderson	Emilie Corcoran	Ann Gimbel
Marilyn Anderson	Donna Crawford	Chris Givens
Sascha Anderson	Christine Cunha	Bonnie Godfred
BrucetteAyoub	Marsha Dahl	Valerie Goodrich
Kathleen Babcock	Kathy Daly	Donna Graffis
June Bagguley	Margie Darlington	Allen Grenn
Jeanette Baird	Paula Day	Kate Hafey
Kathy Barleen	Sally DeMaria	Elizabeth Hanson
Annette Barter	Melinda Dieden	Megan Harmon
Cookie Bedford	Carol Drevno	Janet Harms
Mary Benedict	Marjorie Dunbar	Carol Harris
Dorothea Bergeron	Chris Dunnebier	Martha Harris
Bobbie Besenfelder	Sue Edwards	Melanie Heacock
Jane Beveridge	Stephanie Enna	Chris Hertel
Heidi Bishop	Norma Evans	Linda Hill
Candice Blackman	Penny Fickle	Sharon Hill
Judy Boriskin	Leslie Finta	Eddy Hoffberg
Kathy Bowles	Cindy Fisher	Tina Hogan
Kim Brast	Elizabeth Flynnperrault	Lynn Holligan
Judy Brennan	Chris Fong	Glynis Hood
Jean Brillant	DuBose Forrest	Hilma Jones
Marjorie Briner	Amy Forte	Chris Kaplan
Valerie Briscoe	JoAnn Fossum	Debbie Katz
Pam Brody	Ronni Foy	Diane Kelly
Kris Byrne	Greta Frantz	Cashie Kieckhefer
Chris Cameron	Susan Frost	Karla Kiefert
Susan Caplan	Mary Fuchs	Janet Kleyn-Schoorel
Judy Carney	Roxanne Gahagan	Julie Kolar
Ann Clarkson	Tess Galer	Dale Kyle
Debra Coggins	Sue Gallo	Julie Laird
Jane Collett	Judy Garden	Lena Lamel

Rica Laverda
Cindy Leathers
Heidi Lettis
Eliane Long
Sandi Lutsko
Allyson Lyle
Tim Lynch
Bonnie Macbride
Karen Maggio
Ellen Marienthal
Mary Marraccini
Betty Martin
Lita Mathy
Sheila Matsutani
Judy May
Val Meredith
Sue Migliore
Dixie Mohan
Meredith Mooers
Judy Moore
Suzanne Muraki
Frankie Murray
Linda Murray
Noelle Neighbor
Dorothy Nicholson
Pat Noceti
Kathy Olson
Lani Owyoung
Pam Palitz
Teddy Palmer
Vicki Pappas
Carolyn Poetzsch
Kathy Ramirez
Janice Ray
Kathy Roloff

Bev Rose
Carolyn Rowland
Jennifer Sankey
Jane Scatena
Mary Claire Searby
Cindy Seibert
Denise Sheehan
Dawn Shifreen-Pomerantz
Shirley Siegel
Danielle Signorella
Shayne Silva
Katrina Silvani
Pam Simpson
Kathy Small
Linda Smith
Lynn Snider
Sue Somers
Linda Staaf
Patricia Stapleton
Caren Steffens
Faye Straus
Wendy Sutherland
Fran Taylor
Marcia Thomas
Virginia Tiernan
Marilee Tiras
Alicia Torrey
Alice Turner
Janet Van Etten
Joanne Vance
Jane Walsh
Ellen Walters
Rosamaria Wellman
Kathy Wharton
Anne-Marie Whitney

Mary Kay Wilcock
Debbie Wiley-Bishop
Anne Wondolowski
Roxie Wood
Leota Woods
Irma Wright
Beth Young
Joann Young
Sheila Zainer
Carol Zeman
Mary Zukerberg

*F*or their generous contribution of treasured family recipes, we thank:

Pam Adkins
Rahmi Alameddine
Christel Anderson
Craig Anderson
Karen Anderson
Pam Anderson
Sascha Anderson
Eric Andersson
Garett Andersson
Linda Andersson
Jim Arnold
Laurie Arnold
Jan Askin
Debbie Auwinger
Katia Avila
Brucette Ayoub
Kathleen Babcock
Jeanette Baird
Diane Barbera
Kathy Barleen
Annette Barter
Lis Baston
Cookie Bedford
Lisa Bee-Wilson
Nina Bentley
Donna Black
Carol Blackburn
Candice Blackman
Val Blyth
Linda Bochte
Judy Boriskin
Kathy Bowles

Chris Brahney
Judy Brennan
Jean Brillant
Mary Britton
Pamela Brody
Kelly Brooks
Harriet Burns
Joni Bushnell
Chris Cameron
Marguerite Campione
Susan Caplan
Judy Carney
Jackie Smith Carroll
Barbara Cattolica-Hudson
Dianne Chandler
Terry Choy
Barbara Clark
Nancy Clark
Kathy Clausen
Aaron Clay
Derek Clay
Betty Clogher
Bunny Coffman
Jane Collett
Connie Collier
Sharon Cooley
Jan Cooper
Alice Croft
Ciel Crum
Christine Cunha
Margie Darlington
Sally DeMaria

Sally Devor
Melinda Dieden
Kathy Dimond
Niki Dominguez
Donna Douglas
Sallie Doull
Kathie Dove
Linda Downing
Elizabeth Doyle
Carol Drevno
Sandy Ducey
Wendy Duncan
Karen Dunn-Haley
Chris Dunnebier
Carol Durantini
Judy Ehrhorn
Devra C. Ellert
Pam Elliott
Linda Ellman
Trudy Engeldinger
Stephanie Enna
Rhondda Etheredge
Joan Fernandes
Cindy Ferrell
Debbie Flansburg
DuBose Forrest
Amy Forte
Gina Forte
Ronni Foy
Sharon Fraetis
Greta Frantz
Carol Freitas

Susanne Frey
Susan Frost
Mary Fuchs
Eda Fukayama
Kathy Fulton
Gail Gabriel
Tess Galer
Sue Gallo
Judy Garden
Susan George
Giedra Gershman
Maureen Gillen
Ann Gimbel
Bonnie Godfred
Mitchell Godfred
Anne Marie Gold
Elizabeth Goode
Bethany Haesler
Marzieh Haghighi
Nancy C. Hansen
Jayne Hardin
Sharon Harichandran
Carol Harris
Martha Harris
Sharon Hasegawa
Mike Haverty
Melanie Heacock
Kim Heiser
Kris Hertel
Linda Hill
Eddy Hoffberg
Janet Hoffman
Susan Hoffman
Marilyn Honegger
Scott Honegger

Jill Honeyman
Glynis Hood
Gwynne Hooke
Jeanne Hughes
Terri Huiner
Terri Humann
Pat Hunt
Linda Isola
Marcia Jacober
Glenn Jahnke
Kristin Jahnke
Yvette Jew
Marion Johnson
Hilma Jones
Luise Jones
Shane Jorgensen
Liz Jung
Carla Karsant
Nancy Kassover
Kathleen Keller
Diane Kelly
David Kennedy
Marie Kennedy
Sue Kidd
Bob Kieckhefer
Cashie Kieckhefer
Joannie Kiefer
Roberta Kleoni
Hank Kleyn-Schoorel
Janet Kleyn-Schoorel
Diane Kosak
Karen Kostka
Kelley Kuzak
Mary Sue Kuzak
Susie Lai

Lena Lamel
Patty Landers
Linda Landis
M'Lisa Lawrence
Ginny Leavitt
Martha Lee
Suzette Leith
Wendy Levich
Lynn Lewis
Tina Locke
Sean Lowenthal
Barbara Lussing
Frank Lussing
Julia Lussing
Sandi Lutsko
Allyson Lyle
Tim Lynch
Bonnie Macbride
Karen Maggio
Judie Mahl
Deborah Mahle
John Mara
Linda Mara
Ellen Marienthal
Mary Marraccini
Betty Ann Martin
Susanne Martin
Lita Mathy
Sylvia May
Lynne McClure
Kate McDonald
Alix S. McKenna
Cathy McLin
Val Meredith
Kim Metcalf

Marilyn Miller	Kent Peterman	Patsy Schrupp
Karin Milton	Paige Petersen	Ed Searby
Melissa Moehle	Dan Pinkel	Emily Senturia
Dixie Mohan	Mike Pinkel	Ben Shaw
Linda Momsen	Carolyn Poetzsch	Denise Sheehan
Judy Moore	Carole Price	Mary Ann Shepherd
JoAnne Munley	Edward Price	Dawn Shifreen-Pomerantz
Mark Munley	Anne Raible	Shirley Siegel
Suzanne Muraki	Rosemary Raker	Shayne Silva
Frankie Murray	David Rakip	Katrina Silvani
Linda Murray	Taylor Rakip	Inge Simms
Terry Neifing	Marsha Ramp	Pam Simpson
Noelle Neighbor	Jill Ramsay	Gail Skredynski
Nancy Nelson	Tracey H. Rath	Pete Small
Dorothy Nicholson	Janice Ray	Lynn Smith
Lillie O'Reilly	Carol Reif	Teresa Smith
Kathy Olson	Ana Resnick	Lynn Snider
Sheila Opperman	Susan Rhoades	Linda Staaf
Helen Otten	Gail Riordan	Pam Stark
Jacoba Otten	Shoshana Risman	Faye Straus
Lani Owyoung	Jean Roberts	Martha Strock
Georgia Pack	Cal Robie	Patti Stuckey
Pam King Palitz	Cathy Robie	Tony Suh
Chris Pappageorge	Tia Rogers	Wendy Sutherland
Susie Parker	Beverly Rose	Marilyn Talken
David Peacock	Carolyn Rowland	Cam Teasdale
Jim Peacock	Judy Ryan	Janet Thomas
Jonathan Peacock	Patricia Sallay	Marcia Thomas
Meg Peacock	Virginia Sammann	Beth Thurlow
Robbie Peacock	Chris Saran	Diane Tomkins
Kim-Lien Peck	Laura Sato	Alicia Torrey
Cindy Pelletier	Jane Scatena	Alice Turner
Suzan Pemberton	Susan Schlicher	Jerilou Twohey
JoAnn Perry	Tracy L. Schneider	Pat Van Horn
Maeve Pessis	Louise Schroeter	Dee Vance

Joanne R. Vance
Olive A. Vance
Suzanne Vasgerdsian
Martha Vegvary
Gloria Vetter
Nicole Villata
Mary Walden
Kathleen Walsh
Ellen Walters
Ann Ward
Mitch Ward
Marcia Waterbury

Anne Webster
Marcia Welch
Rosamaria Wellman
Susan Welty
Carol Wendell
Carolyn West
Kathy Wharton
Gail Wherritt
Nancy White
Ann-Marie Whitney
Debbie Wihera
Debbie Wiley-Bishop

Alyce Windhurst
Bruce Wodhams
Maureen Wong
Roxie Wood
Leota Woods
Bill Wright
Irma Wright
Sue Yamashita
Judy Yoakum
Beth Young
Carol Zeman

T he sale of *The Lafayette Collection* will return over $100,000 directly to the children of the Lafayette School District. Before it could be published, however, it was necessary to raise enough money to cover all of the expenses connected with the project. This happened through the generosity and support of the Page Sponsors listed below as well as the businesses and families listed in the honor rolls at the end of the book.

Adams & Company, Lafayette

Alpine Dental Care, Martinez

American Protective Services, Inc., Oakland

The Jon Andron Family

A•Plumbing Company, Lafayette

Athens Benefits Insurance Services, Concord

Patty Battersby, Solomon Wilmington Real Estate, Orinda

Bay Area Physical Therapy Center, Lafayette

Bay Area Travel Company, Lafayette

Bear Forest Properties

Bedford Properties, Lafayette

The Clay Bentley Family

Better Homes Realty, Lafayette

Bill's Drugs, Lafayette

Blodgett's Carpet & Linoleum, Lafayette

The Joel Boriskin Family

Brillant and Associates, Lafayette

Brooks Typography, Lafayette

John A. Brown Kitchenwares, Oakland

Buckley, Patchen, Riemann & Phillips, Lafayette

Burton Valley Elementary School Faculty & Staff

Butler-Conti Dodge, Lafayette

C.C. Ole's Mexican Restaurant, Concord

Fiesta Paints, Lafayette
Fleming Companies, Inc., Milpitas
Floral Arts Florist, Lafayette
Foley, McIntosh & Foley, Lafayette
Freddie's Pizza, Lafayette
Friend of the Cookbook
Friend of the Cookbook
Friend of the Cookbook
Friend of the Cookbook
Friend of the Cookbook
Friend of the Cookbook
Friend of the Cookbook
Friend of the Cookbook
Friend of the Cookbook
Friend of the Cookbook
Friend of the Cookbook
Friend of the Cookbook
Friend of the Cookbook
Friend of the Cookbook
Friend of the Cookbook
Geppetto's Cafe, Lafayette
Global International, Walnut Creek
The Grapevine, Lafayette
Great Wall Restaurant, Lafayette
Marianne Greene, Solomon Wilmington Real Estate, Orinda
The Marshall Grodin Family
Guy's Drugs, Lafayette
Happy Days Learning Center, Lafayette
Happy Valley Elementary School Staff
Happy Valley Improvement Association
Mr. & Mrs. Cal Hatch
The Donald Heacock Family
Hickey & Hill, Inc., Lafayette
Allan R. Horeis Structural Engineers, Walnut Creek

The David Howerton Family
Douglas J. Hudson, D.D.S., Orthodontics, Moraga
The Eliot Hudson Family
Humann Company, Lafayette
Lawrence Johnson & Associates, Oakland
Ian B. Johnston, M.D., Walnut Creek
The Mark Jones Family
KRT Marketing, Lafayette
Kaffee Barbara Cafe-Restaurant, Lafayette
James B. Karol, M.D., Oakland & Alameda
Kelly Tama Shiffman, Inc., Walnut Creek
Jeanne's Hamlin Cleaners, Lafayette
Lafayette Ace Hardware
Lafayette Book Store
Lafayette Chamber of Commerce
Lafayette Education Association
Lafayette Elementry School Teachers
Lafayette Exxon
Lafayette Garden Club
Lafayette School District Administrative Council
Lafayette School District Governing Board
Lafayette Shell Service
Lafayette Tennis Club
Mr. & Mrs. Arthur Laibly
Lamorinda National Bank, Lafayette
Lamorinda Pediatrics, Lafayette
Lamorinda Veterinary Hospital, Lafayette
The John Layng Family
Lescure Company, Inc., Lafayette
J. Linneman & Company, San Francisco
The Peter Locke Family
Longs Drug Stores, Contra Costa County
Luciani-Schlatter & Associates, San Francisco
Lucky Stores, Inc.

Rosewood House, Oakland & Concord
Susan Rothenberg, TRI Realtors, Orinda
Roughing It Day Camp, Lafayette
Round Table Pizza, Lafayette
Round Up Saloon, Lafayette
Safeway, Inc., Fremont
Charles M. Salter Associates, Inc., San Francisco
Dr. & Mrs. John Salzman
Jon E. Sammann, D.D.S., Orthodontics, Lafayette
Michael J. Sayegh, D.D.S., Lafayette
The Rex Scatena Family
Barbara Shaw Seminars, Lafayette
Sierra Boat Company, Carnelian Bay
Simon Home Center, Walnut Creek
Barclay Simpson Fine Arts Gallery, Lafayette
The Wallace Slough Family
J. Craig Smith, D.V.M., Moraga
The Charles Snyder Family
Springhill Elementary School Staff
Staglin Family Vineyard, Lafayette
Stanley Intermediate School P.T.A.
Katherine Jernberg and Stephen Stanley
R.T. Steffens, TRI Real Estate Services, Walnut Creek
The Storyteller, Lafayette
William L. Strauss, M.D., Moraga
Supercuts, Moraga
Supercuts, Sacramento
The Wendy Sutherland Family
Kenneth Sutherland Co., Oakland
Taco Bell, Lafayette
Take One Video, Lafayette
Taylor Made Office Systems, Inc., Concord
J. Christopher Thompson, D.D.S., Inc., Walnut Creek
Toyko Chicken Restaurant, Lafayette

Twigs, Lafayette
Ann Hudspeth Ward, Coldwell Banker, Orinda
Carolyn Way, John M. Grubb Realtors, Orinda
Wells Fargo Bank, Lafayette
Western Data Group, Lafayette
Westinghouse Electric Corporation, Lafayette
The Steven Whitney Family
Roger and Kit Wiggins
The Paul Yeomans Family

Table of Contents

APPETIZERS

Torte Milanese
Vegetable Fritatta
Baked Farm Cheese with Fresh Tomatoes and Herbs
California Calzone
Sausage Spinach Wreath
Mushroom Croustades
Havarti en Croûte
Gyoza - Japanese Pot Stickers
Tequila Lime Shrimp
Dijon Chicken Wings
Sticky Chicken
Tortellini in Herb-Garlic Dressing
Spinach Artichoke Dip
Lemon Cheese Ball
Crab Dip
Gazpacho Salsa
Chili Cheese Shrimp
Tapenade

Page sponsored by Lafayette Suburban Junior Women's Club

Torte Milanese

2 bunches Swiss chard, stems removed
3 red bell peppers, cut in strips
1 package frozen puff pastry
1 pound ham, thinly sliced
1 pound Swiss cheese, thinly sliced
1 egg, well beaten

Preheat oven to 350º F.

Separately blanch the chard and peppers until tender. Drain and dry each thoroughly. Butter the bottom and sides of a 9" springform pan. Roll out one sheet of pastry dough until it is large enough to fit into the pan, covering the bottom and sides and leaving a 1/2" overhang. Fit the pastry into the pan. Layer, in order, ham, chard, cheese and peppers. Repeat the layering. Roll out the remaining sheet of puff pastry. Cut it into a 10" circle and place on top of the torte. Crimp the edges together to seal tightly. Use the remaining pastry to decorate the torte.

Bake for 45 minutes on the middle rack of the oven. Remove and brush pastry with egg. Bake for an additional 15 minutes until golden brown. Let stand until just warm. Garnish and serve in slices.

———————— ❧ ————————

Vegetable Fritatta

12 ounces marinated artichoke hearts,
   drained, reserving 1/2 the marinade
1 onion, chopped
2 cloves garlic, minced
1 tomato, seeded and chopped
2 zucchini, finely chopped
2 eggs, beaten
1/2 cup Bisquick
2 tablespoons minced fresh parsley
2 cups grated cheddar cheese
1/2 teaspoon oregano
Salt and pepper

Preheat oven to 325° F.

Chop the artichoke hearts. In a large skillet, heat the reserved marinade and add the artichoke hearts, onion, garlic, tomato, and zucchini. Sauté approximately 10 minutes, until the onion and zucchini are cooked. Remove from the heat.

In a bowl, combine the eggs, Bisquick, parsley, cheese, and seasonings. Add to the sautéed vegetables and mix well. Pour into a greased 9" square baking dish.

Bake until lightly browned and set, approximately 30 minutes. Cool to room temperature. Cut into small squares and serve.

NOTE: This may be made ahead and served cold.

Baked Farm Cheese
with Fresh Tomatoes and Herbs
From Cafe P.M. at Nordstrom

Farm Cheese

1 pound cream cheese, softened to
    room temperature
1/2 bunch fresh basil, finely chopped
1/2 bunch fresh parsley,
    finely chopped
1 tablespoon dry oregano
1/2 teaspoon freshly ground black
    pepper

Tomato-Basil Sauce

6 fresh whole tomatoes,
    scored, stems removed
1 tablespoon olive oil
1 tablespoon minced garlic
1/4 cup white wine
Salt and pepper to taste
1/2 bunch fresh basil,
    coarsely chopped

Cheese: Combine all cheese ingredients and set aside.

Sauce: Blanch the tomatoes in boiling water for 2 minutes. Remove from the heat and immediately immerse the tomatoes in ice water. Remove skin and discard. Core and quarter the tomatoes.

Heat the oil and sauté the garlic until lightly browned. Add the wine and reduce for 1 minute. Add the tomatoes, salt, pepper and continue cooking for 15 minutes. Remove from heat and add the fresh basil.

Preheat broiler.

Ladle the sauce onto an ovenproof serving platter. Shape the farm cheese into a round, flat patty. Center the cheese on top of the sauce and broil 5-10 minutes until browned. Serve with garlic toast triangles.

California Calzone

1 pound Bridgeford frozen bread
   dough, thawed
8 ounces ricotta cheese
1 teaspoon oregano
1 tablespoon minced fresh parsley
1/2 teaspoon thyme
3/4 cup diced ham
1 tomato, seeded and chopped
4 ounces mozzarella cheese, grated
4 ounces cheddar cheese, grated

Preheat oven to 350º F.

On a lightly floured surface, roll bread dough into a large rectangle, no more than 1/3" thick. Transfer to a large ungreased cookie sheet.

Combine the ricotta with the herbs. Spread the mixture lengthwise down the middle third of the dough, leaving approximately 3" of dough showing at each end. On top of the ricotta mixture, layer the ham, tomato, mozzarella and cheddar. Fold the 3" ends over the filling. Then fold the sides up over the filling and pinch them together. You should now have a long rectangular loaf.

Bake for approximately 30 minutes or until the bread is golden brown. Slice and serve warm.

NOTE: This is also good served in larger slices as a light entree. Use your imagination with the filling -- mushrooms, olives, sausage, etc.

Sausage Spinach Wreath

12 ounces seasoned bulk pork sausage
1 loaf Bridgeford frozen bread dough, thawed
10 ounces frozen chopped spinach, thawed
1 cup cheddar cheese, grated
Garlic powder

Preheat oven to 350º F.

In a skillet, cook the sausage, breaking it into small pieces. Drain well and set aside.

On a lightly floured surface, roll out the bread dough into a 13" x 8" rectangle. Layer with sausage, spinach and cheese. Sprinkle with garlic powder. Beginning with one of the long sides, roll it up like a jelly roll. Place the seam side down onto a greased cookie sheet and bend it into a wreath. Pinch the ends together.

Bake for 20-25 minutes, until golden brown. Slice and serve.

Mushroom Croustades

Croustades

1 loaf of firm white bread
Butter, melted

Filling

2 tablespoons water

2 tablespoons lemon juice

2 tablespoons chopped chives

3 tablespoons minced green onions

4 tablespoons butter

1/2 pound fresh mushrooms, minced

2 tablespoons flour

1 cup half & half

1/2 teaspoon cayenne pepper

2 teaspoons chopped fresh parsley

Preheat oven to 350º F.

Croustades: Trim the crusts off the bread and flatten each piece with a rolling pin. Cut each piece into 4 squares. Using a small muffin tin, put approximately 1/2 teaspoon of butter and one square of bread into each muffin cup. Gently press each square of bread, molding it into the cup. Bake until browned, 8-10 minutes.

Filling: Combine the water, lemon juice and chives. Set aside. Sauté the onions in butter. Add the mushrooms and cook for 10-15 minutes or until moisture is gone. Remove from the heat and sprinkle with flour, stirring until well blended. Return to the heat, add the half & half and bring to a boil. Simmer for 2 minutes. Remove from the heat. Drain the chives. Add pepper, parsley and chives to the mushroom mixture. Mix well and cool.

Fill the croustades with filling. Return to the oven, heat thoroughly and serve. Makes approximately 48.

Page sponsored by a Friend of the Cookbook
In honor of Marcia Thomas

Havarti en Croûte

2 frozen Pepperidge Farm pastry shells
7 ounces Havarti cheese with dill
1 egg, lightly beaten
Apples

Let the pastry shells thaw slightly. Stack them on a lightly floured board and roll them out into an 8" circle. Place the cheese in the center of the pastry. Bring the edges together over the top of the cheese, and pinch together to seal. Place on an ungreased cookie sheet, brush with the egg and chill for 1 hour.

Preheat oven to 375º F.

Brush again with the egg. Bake for 15-20 minutes, until golden brown. While still warm, cut into wedges and serve with apple slices.

VARIATION: Also delicious substituting Brie or Camembert with green onions, almonds or pecans.

Gyoza
Japanese Pot Stickers

3/4 pound lean ground pork
1/2 pound bay shrimp
10 ounces frozen chopped spinach,
   thawed and squeezed
5 mushrooms, minced
1 tablespoon chopped green onion
1 teaspoon grated fresh ginger
2 tablespoons soy sauce
2 tablespoons sesame oil
1 package gyoza wrappers*

Mix all ingredients except the wrappers together. Spoon approximately 1 teaspoon of the mixture onto the middle of a gyoza wrapper. Dip a finger in a bowl of water and "draw" a line around the edge of the wrapper. Fold over into a semi-circle and pinch to close. Repeat this process, filling all of the wrappers.

In a large frying pan, heat a thin layer of oil over medium heat. Add the gyoza to the pan, a few at a time, and brown on both sides. Add 1/3 cup water to the pan, being careful of splattering oil. Cover and steam for approximately 5 minutes or until the water has evaporated. Keep warm in a flat glass casserole dish. Repeat this process until all pot stickers are cooked.

To serve, sprinkle with soy sauce and sesame oil. You may also sprinkle on a bit of chili oil for a hot, spicy touch.

Makes approximately 20.

*Gyoza wrappers are similar to wonton wrappers but are round.

Page sponsored by Simon Home Center, Walnut Creek 935-8100

Tequila Lime Shrimp

2 pounds large shrimp, unpeeled
1/4 cup fresh lime juice
1/4 cup tequila
2 garlic cloves, minced
2 shallots, finely chopped
2 teaspoons cumin
1 teaspoon salt
1/2 teaspoon pepper
1/2 cup olive oil
Lime slices
Fresh cilantro

Soak bamboo skewers in water for at least 1 hour. This will prevent them from splintering and burning when grilled.

Thread 3 shrimp on each skewer. Lay the skewered shrimp in a shallow, non-aluminum dish, large enough to hold them in a single layer.

Whisk together the lime juice, tequila, garlic, shallots, cumin, salt, and pepper. Slowly add the oil, whisking until combined. Taste for seasonings.

Pour this mixture over the shrimp and marinate 2-4 hours. Grill the shrimp on each side for approximately 4 minutes. On individual plates, arrange 2 skewers garnished with lime slices and fresh cilantro.

Dijon Chicken Wings

1/2 cup Dijon mustard
1/4 cup soy sauce
1/4 cup vegetable oil
6 cloves garlic, minced
20 chicken wings

Combine mustard, soy sauce, oil and garlic. Place the chicken wings in a baking dish and cover with the marinade. Marinate *overnight* in the refrigerator.

Preheat oven to 350º F.

Bake the chicken in the marinade for approximately 1 hour, turning occasionally.

NOTE: These are delicious served hot or cold.

Page sponsored by Wells Fargo Bank, Lafayette 284-9100

Sticky Chicken

1 cup soy sauce

1 cup white wine vinegar

3/4 cup sugar

4 cloves garlic, minced

4 green onions, chopped

2 tablespoons grated fresh ginger

30 chicken drumettes

In a large bowl, combine the soy sauce, vinegar, and sugar, stirring until the sugar dissolves. Add the garlic, green onions, ginger and mix well. Arrange the chicken in a glass dish and cover with the marinade to coat. Refrigerate **overnight**, stirring occasionally.

Pour the chicken and marinade into a large skillet or wok. Cook over medium heat until the liquid evaporates and forms a sticky coating on the chicken, approximately 45 minutes. Do not overcook or the chicken will fall off the bones. Serve hot or at room temperature.

Page sponsored by Rosewood House, Fine Oriental Furniture
Oakland 451-7373 and Concord 827-9588

Tortellini in Herb-Garlic Dressing

1 pound tortellini
1/4 cup red wine vinegar
3/4 cup olive oil
1 clove garlic, minced
1 tablespoon Dijon mustard
Salt and pepper
8 fresh basil leaves, finely chopped
2 tablespoons chopped fresh parsley
4 green onions, finely chopped
Cherry tomatoes or red bell peppers
1/2 cup freshly grated parmesan cheese

Cook the tortellini al dente. Drain it and rinse with cold water. Place it in a bowl.

Whisk the vinegar and oil together until well blended. Whisk in the garlic, mustard, salt and pepper. Pour the mixture over the tortellini. Add the basil, parsley, green onions and toss gently. Serve on skewers alternating with red pepper squares or cherry tomatoes. Top with parmesan cheese.

Page sponsored by Ann Hudspeth Ward
Coldwell Banker Real Estate, Orinda 254-7850

Spinach Artichoke Dip

10 ounces frozen chopped spinach, thawed
14 ounces canned artichoke hearts (not marinated)
4 ounces canned diced green chilies
1 cup mayonnaise
1 cup freshly grated parmesan cheese
1/4 teaspoon garlic powder

Preheat oven to 325° F.

Squeeze the liquid from the spinach. Drain the artichoke hearts and cut them into eighths. Carefully mix all of the ingredients. Pour mixture into a 9" quiche dish.

Bake for 15 minutes, stirring twice. Place under the broiler for about 1 minute until the top is lightly browned. Serve with tortilla chips.

Page sponsored by Chevron Corporation, San Ramon

Lemon Cheese Ball

8 ounces cream cheese, softened
1 teaspoon grated lemon rind
1 1/2 teaspoons lemon juice
1 tablespoon powdered sugar
Chopped almonds
Pears
Apples
Jicama

Combine the cream cheese, lemon rind, lemon juice, sugar and form into a ball. Roll in the chopped almonds. Chill **overnight**. Serve at room temperature spread on slices of pears, apples and jicama.

Page sponsored by The Grapevine, Lafayette 284-2651

Crab Dip

8 ounces cream cheese, softened
1 pound fresh crab meat
1 cup mayonnaise
1/2 cup sour cream
1/8 teaspoon soy sauce
2 cloves garlic, minced
1 tablespoon Worcestershire sauce
1/4 teaspoon Tabasco sauce
2 teaspoons lemon juice
Dash of cayenne pepper

Beat the cream cheese until it is smooth. Stir in the remaining ingredients.
Refrigerate **overnight** to allow the flavors to blend. Serve with baguette slices
or crackers.

~

Page sponsored by Mary McDonald
Mason McDuffie, Orinda 254-0440 or 284-4429

Gazpacho Salsa

32 ounces stewed tomatoes
12 ounces tomato paste
4 ounces chopped olives
6 ounces canned sliced mushrooms
4 ounces canned diced jalapeños
1/3 cup finely chopped onion
3 cloves garlic, minced
2 tablespoons vinegar
2 tablespoons vegetable oil

Pour the stewed tomatoes with juices into a large earthenware bowl (not metal or plastic). Chop the tomatoes into smaller pieces. Add all other ingredients and mix well. Chill at least 12 hours to blend the flavors. Serve with tortilla chips.

NOTE: This is quite hot! It is also very good as a thick salsa for Mexican dishes or cheese omelets.

Chili Cheese Shrimp

16 ounces cream cheese, softened
2 tablespoons Worcestershire sauce
1/4 teaspoon grated lemon peel
1 tablespoon lemon juice
1/2 cup sliced green onion
1/8 teaspoon Tabasco sauce
12 ounces bottled chili sauce
1 tablespoon horseradish
12 ounces small cooked shrimp

In a bowl, beat the first 6 ingredients together until smooth. Spread into the bottom of a shallow one quart dish.

Mix the chili sauce and horseradish. Spread this over the cream cheese mixture.

Top with shrimp. Serve cold with crackers.

Page sponsored by American Protective Services, Inc., Oakland 568-0276

Tapenade

20 oil cured black olives*
2 garlic cloves, minced
4 anchovy fillets, drained
2 tablespoons capers, well drained
2 teaspoons Dijon mustard
2 tablespoons fresh lemon juice
2 tablespoons finely chopped fresh basil
1/4 cup finely chopped Italian parsley
1/8 teaspoon cayenne pepper
1/2 cup olive oil
Lemon slices
Sprigs of fresh parsley

Place the olives on a breadboard and smash them with the back of a heavy cleaver, separating the pit from the olive. Discard the pits.

Combine all ingredients, except the olive oil, lemon slices and parsley sprigs, in a food processor. Process until smooth. With the motor running, slowly add the oil until it is completely absorbed. Refrigerate until ready to serve.

Garnish with lemon slices and sprigs of parsley and serve with crackers.

NOTE: This may be prepared up to one week ahead. It is excellent as a topping for fish or pasta.

*Kalamata olives are suggested and are available at delis and specialty food stores.

SOUPS & SALADS

Fresh Asparagus Soup
Broccoli Bisque
Sherried Carrot Soup
Cream of Mushroom Soup
Onion Soup Gratinée
Watercress Soup
Journey's End Vegetable Soup
Mexican Bean Soup
Barley Prosciutto Soup
Chicken Rice Soup
Gingery Chicken Soup
Red Snapper Soup
Harvest Salmon Chowder
Seafood Gazpacho
Insalata alla Parmigiana
Orange Almond Salad
Curried Spinach Salad
NY Deli Slaw
Oriental Cabbage Salad
Cucumber Salad
Green Beans with Mustard Vinaigrette
Greek Tomato Salad
Basque Pickled Beans
Russian Salad
German Potato Salad
Artichoke Rice Salad
Confetti Rice Salad
Tortellini Salad

Cilantro Chicken Salad
Curry Salad
Chinese Chicken Salad
Tokyo Chicken's Salad Dressing
Celery Seed Dressing
Blue Cheese Dressing
Dilled Louis Dressing
Green Goddess Dressing

Fresh Asparagus Soup

1 pound fresh asparagus

4 bacon strips

1 large shallot, chopped

2 leeks, whites only, thinly sliced

1 clove garlic, chopped

1 tablespoon flour

3 1/2 cups chicken broth

1 russet potato, peeled and cubed

1 cup half & half

Separate asparagus tips and stems and blanch both in boiling water for
2 minutes. Drain and reserve the tips. Cut the stems into one inch lengths.

In a large stock pot, sauté the bacon until crisp. Remove the bacon to a paper
towel. Drain the drippings, leaving approximately 2 tablespoons in the pot.
Add the shallots, leeks, garlic and sauté for approximately 15 minutes. Sprinkle
in the flour and stir to blend. Slowly add the broth, stirring continuously. Add
the asparagus stems and potato. Bring to a boil. Reduce heat, cover and simmer
for 30 minutes or until the potatoes are fully cooked.

Purée the soup in batches in a blender or food processor. Return soup to the
stock pot, add the half & half and stir to heat thoroughly.

Garnish with crumbled bacon and reserved asparagus tips.

Serves 4-6.

Broccoli Bisque

2 bunches fresh broccoli, chopped
1/2 cup chopped onion
4 cups chicken broth
4 tablespoons butter
2 tablespoons flour
2 teaspoons salt
Dash of white pepper
1 lemon
4 cups half & half
Sour cream
Bacon, crumbled

In a stock pot, combine the broccoli, onion and broth.   Bring to a boil, reduce heat and simmer uncovered for 10 minutes. Purée in batches in a blender or food processor until smooth. Set aside.

In the stock pot, melt the butter. Add the flour, salt, pepper and a squeeze of lemon. Stir until smooth. Stir in the half & half. Add the broccoli mixture and heat thoroughly.

Garnish with a dollop of sour cream and the bacon.

Sherried Carrot Soup

2 cups chicken broth
1 pound carrots, peeled and sliced
1 onion, chopped
1/4 teaspoon curry powder
Dash of nutmeg
Salt and pepper
1 cup half & half
1/4 cup sherry
Sour cream
Italian parsley

In a medium saucepan, bring the chicken broth, carrots and onions to a simmer. When the vegetables are tender, remove from the heat and purée in a blender or food processor until smooth. Return to the saucepan and add curry powder, nutmeg, salt, pepper, half & half and sherry. Blend over low heat until warm. Soup should be a bit thick.

Garnish with sour cream and Italian parsley.

Serves 4-6.

Page sponsored by Barbara Shaw Seminars, Lafayette 283-6929
In honor of Stacey's first principal

Cream of Mushroom Soup

1 pound mushrooms
1 onion, finely chopped
5 cups chicken broth
3 tablespoons butter
3 tablespoons flour
1 cup heavy cream
1/2 teaspoon salt
Dash of cayenne
Parsley

Chop the mushroom stems. Slice and reserve the mushroom caps. In a saucepan, place the stems, onion and broth and simmer for 20 minutes. Strain the broth. In a medium saucepan, melt the butter and stir in the flour. Slowly add the broth and whisk until smooth. Add sliced mushrooms, cream, salt and cayenne. Simmer 10 minutes.

Garnish with parsley.

Serves 6.

Page sponsored by The Great Wall Restaurant, Lafayette 284-3500

Onion Soup Gratinée

Soup
8 yellow onions, thinly sliced
4 tablespoons butter
1 tablespoon olive oil
1/4 teaspoon salt
1 teaspoon sugar
1/4 cup flour
8 cups chicken or beef stock
1/4 cup dry white wine
2 tablespoons brandy
Salt and pepper
Croutons (recipe included)
Sliced Gruyère or Swiss cheese

Croutons
1/4 inch slices of
   French bread
Olive oil
Garlic cloves

Soup: In a covered saucepan, slowly cook the onions in butter and oil for 25-30 minutes, stirring often. Add the salt and sugar and continue cooking, uncovered for 1 hour or until golden. Stir in the flour and cook 5 minutes. In a separate pan, bring the stock to a boil and add onion mixture and wine. Bring back to a boil. Reduce the heat, cover and simmer for 45 minutes. Before serving, add brandy, salt and pepper.

Croutons: Brush the bread with oil and rub with cut cloves of garlic. Toast on broiler pan until golden, turning once.

Fill crocks or ovenproof bowls with the soup and place a crouton on top. Top with cheese and broil until the cheese is brown and bubbly.

Serves 6-8.

Page sponsored by Lescure Company, Inc., Lafayette 283-2528

Watercress Soup

5 tablespoons butter

2 leeks, white and tender green parts sliced

3 cups watercress, stems removed

3 medium potatoes, peeled and sliced

1/2 teaspoon salt

1/4 teaspoon pepper

3 cups water

1 1/2 cups chicken broth

3/4 cup half & half

In a medium saucepan, melt 2 tablespoons of the butter and sauté the leeks until soft. Add watercress and sauté gently until limp but not browned. Add the potatoes, salt, pepper, water, broth and bring to boil. Reduce the heat and simmer uncovered 15 minutes. Cool slightly and purée in a blender or food processor until smooth. Return to the pan and heat over medium heat, adding half & half. Swirl in remaining butter and serve.

Serves 6.

Page sponsored by Momsen Construction & Development Co., Lafayette
Jeff, Linda, Nick & Paige Momsen

Journey's End Vegetable Soup

1/4 cup butter	2/3 cup diced potatoes
1/2 cup diced carrot	1/3 cup diced turnip
1/2 cup diced onion	1/4 cup cooked red kidney beans*
1/2 cup diced celery	1/4 cup cooked navy or lima beans*
1/4 teaspoon oregano	1/2 cup macaroni
1/4 teaspoon Italian herb seasoning	1 tablespoon chopped fresh parsley
1/8 teaspoon basil	1 tablespoon barley*
1/8 teaspoon thyme	1 tablespoon green split peas*
1/8 teaspoon rosemary	1 tablespoon lentils*
1 clove garlic, minced	1 cup chopped spinach
1 bay leaf	1/2 cup chopped cabbage
7 cups beef stock	Salt and pepper
1 cup canned tomatoes, drained	

In a large saucepan, melt the butter over medium heat. Add the next ten ingredients and cook, stirring frequently, until the vegetables soften, approximately 8 minutes. Add the remaining ingredients except the spinach and cabbage. Cover and simmer 40 minutes. Add the spinach and cabbage and cook an additional 10 minutes. Serve immediately.

Serves 6-8.

*Pre-packaged mixed beans may be used in place of kidney and lima beans, barley, split peas and lentils.

Mexican Bean Soup

4 pounds boneless pork, diced
1 cup chopped onion
4 cloves garlic, chopped
2 tablespoons vegetable oil
4 tablespoons chili powder
1 tablespoon oregano
2 tablespoons ground cumin
8 cups water
5 1/4 cups beef broth
2 cups dry pinto beans
4 cups carrots, peeled and thinly sliced
2 large jars baby corn cobs (pickled are best)
Cilantro
Tomatoes
Sour cream

In a large stock pot, brown the pork, onions and garlic in oil. Add the chili powder, oregano, cumin, water, broth and beans. Simmer uncovered for several hours. When the meat and beans are tender, add the carrots. When the carrots are tender, add the corn. Serve hot.

Garnish with chopped cilantro, tomatoes and a dollop of sour cream.

Makes 6 quarts.

Barley Prosciutto Soup

1/4 cup butter

1/4 cup finely chopped shallots

1 cup pearl barley

6 cups chicken broth

1/4 pound prosciutto, cut into thin ribbons

1/4 teaspoon pepper

1 cup heavy cream

10 ounces frozen petite peas, thawed

1 cup freshly grated parmesan cheese

1 whole nutmeg

In a 5-6 quart stock pot, melt the butter and sauté the shallots until limp. Add the barley and sauté until golden. Stir in the broth, prosciutto and pepper. Bring to a boil. Reduce the heat, cover and simmer until the barley is tender, approximately 30 minutes. Add the cream and peas. Heat thoroughly. Top with parmesan cheese and freshly grated nutmeg.

Serves 6-8.

Chicken Rice Soup

4 chicken breast halves, skinned

8 cups water

2 stalks celery, chopped

1 large carrot, grated

1 medium onion, chopped

2 tablespoons vegetable oil

3 chicken bouillon cubes

3/4 cup long grain rice

1 tablespoon lemon juice

1 teaspoon salt

1/2 teaspoon thyme

1/4 teaspoon pepper

Cook the chicken in water until tender, about 20 minutes. Remove the chicken and cool, reserving broth. Cut the chicken into bite-size pieces.

In a skillet, cook the celery, carrot and onion in oil until tender. Add the vegetables to the broth with all remaining ingredients except the chicken and simmer for 20 minutes or until the rice is cooked. Add the chicken and heat thoroughly.

Serves 8-10.

Gingery Chicken Soup

3 chicken breast halves
6 cups water
1 1/2 teaspoons salt
3 tablespoons freshly grated ginger root
3 green onions, sliced diagonally
1 cup mushrooms, sliced
8 1/2 ounces canned water chestnuts, drained and diced
1 teaspoon soy sauce
1 cup shredded lettuce

In a large saucepan, combine the chicken, water, salt and ginger. Bring to a boil. Reduce the heat, cover and simmer 30 minutes or until tender. Remove the chicken and cool slightly. Strain the broth and return it to the saucepan to simmer. When the chicken is cool, skin, bone, and cut it into chunks.

Skim the fat from the broth. Strain the broth again and return it to the saucepan to simmer. Add the green onions, mushrooms, water chestnuts, soy sauce and chicken. Simmer for 10 minutes. Stir in the lettuce just before serving.

Serves 6.

—————————— ❧ ——————————

Red Snapper Soup

Fish Stock
1/2 pound of fish
1-2 quarts of water
1 onion, quartered

Brown Sauce
5 tablespoons butter
3 shallots, finely chopped
1 cup red wine
1 1/4 cups beef broth
1 teaspoon tarragon
Pinch of thyme
3 tablespoons flour

Soup
1/2 cup diced onion
1/2 cup diced celery
1 cup diced green pepper
2 tablespoons butter
4 cups fresh fish stock (recipe included)
1/2 cup plus 2 tablespoons sherry wine
1 cup red snapper fillet, diced
2 cups tomato sauce
4 cups brown sauce (recipe included)
1 teaspoon Worcestershire sauce
1/2 teaspoon salt

Stock: Combine the fish with the water and onions. Simmer 20-30 minutes. Strain before using.

Sauce: In a medium saucepan, melt 3 tablespoons of the butter and sauté the shallots. Gradually add the wine, broth and bring to a boil. Add the tarragon and thyme. Reduce by half. In a small saucepan, melt the remaining butter and mix in the flour to make a paste. Gradually add the paste to the sauce to thicken it to desired consistency. Strain.

Soup: In a large saucepan, melt the butter and sauté the onions, celery and green peppers until the onions are translucent. Add the fish stock and 1/2 cup of the sherry. Cook over low heat for 25 minutes. Add the red snapper and cook an additional 10 minutes. Add the tomato sauce, brown sauce, Worcestershire sauce, salt and simmer 5 minutes. Lace the soup with the remaining sherry and serve immediately.

Serves 6-8.

Harvest Salmon Chowder

3 tablespoons butter

1/2 cup chopped onion

1/2 cup chopped celery

1/4 cup chopped green pepper

1 clove garlic, minced

1 cup diced potatoes

1 cup diced carrots

2 cups chicken broth

3/4 teaspoon pepper

1 teaspoon salt

1/2 teaspoon dill weed

1/2 cup diced zucchini

7 3/4 ounces canned salmon,
    drained and flaked, reserving liquid

13 ounces evaporated milk

8 3/4 ounces cream style corn

Chopped fresh parsley

In a large saucepan, melt the butter and sauté the onion, celery, green pepper and garlic until tender. Add the potatoes, carrots, broth and seasonings. Cover and simmer 20 minutes. Add the zucchini and cook an additional 5 minutes. Add the salmon, reserved liquid, evaporated milk and corn. Heat thoroughly. Sprinkle with parsley.

Serves 4 as a main dish.

Page sponsored by L. N. Curtis & Sons, Oakland
The Curtis Family

Seafood Gazpacho

1 quart Clamato juice
1/2 cup cucumber, peeled and chopped
1/3 cup green onion, thinly sliced
1 avocado, coarsely chopped
1 cup tomato juice
2 tablespoons olive oil
2 tablespoons red wine vinegar
1 teaspoon sugar
1 teaspoon dill
1 clove garlic, crushed
1/4 teaspoon Tabasco sauce
1/2 pound bay shrimp
Dash lemon juice
Salt and pepper
Chives

Combine the first 11 ingredients in a large glass serving bowl. Add the bay shrimp and lemon juice. Season with salt and pepper.

Chill well, preferably **overnight.**

Garnish with fresh chopped chives.

Serves 8.

NOTE: The shrimp will turn very pink from Clamato juice.

Insalata alla Parmigiana

3/4 cup olive oil

1/2 cup red wine vinegar

2 cloves garlic, crushed

1 ounce pimientos, chopped

1/3 medium red onion, grated

1/2 head Romaine lettuce, torn and chilled

1 head leaf lettuce, torn and chilled

1 cup hearts of palm, sliced

1 cup marinated artichoke hearts, cut in half

1 medium red onion, thinly sliced

2 cups freshly grated Parmesan cheese

In a bowl, mix the oil, vinegar, garlic, pimiento and grated onion. Chill for several hours.

In a salad bowl combine the lettuce, hearts of palm, artichokes and sliced onions. Add the dressing and at least 1 cup of the Parmesan cheese. Toss lightly. Chill for 15-20 minutes. This salad must sit to enhance the flavor. Serve with more Parmesan cheese.

NOTE: This salad should look like it is coated with Parmesan. The dressing should not be visible.

Page sponsored by Brillant and Associates, Life & Health Insurance, Lafayette 283-5810
In support of The Lafayette Schools

Orange Almond Salad

Poppy Seed Dressing
2 tablespoons onion, grated
1/2 cup sugar
1 teaspoon poppy seeds
1 teaspoon Dijon mustard
1/2 cup white wine vinegar
3/4 cup safflower oil
1 tablespoon mayonnaise
Salt

Salad
1 head Bibb lettuce, torn into bite-size pieces
1 red onion, thinly sliced
11 ounces canned Mandarin orange slices, chilled
1/4 cup almond slivers, toasted
1/2 cup crumbled blue cheese

Place the first 4 dressing ingredients in a blender or food processor. Blend until smooth. Add the vinegar and blend again. With the machine running, slowly add oil. Blend in the mayonnaise and season with salt. Chill for at least 1 hour to allow the flavors to blend.

Combine all salad ingredients in a bowl or arrange decoratively on six individual plates. Add the dressing and serve.

Page sponsored by The Howerton Family

Curried Spinach Salad

Dressing

1/2 cup white wine vinegar

2/3 cup vegetable oil

1 tablespoon Major Grey Chutney, finely chopped

1 teaspoon curry powder

1 teaspoon dry mustard

1/2 teaspoon salt

1/4 teaspoon Tabasco sauce

Salad

3 bunches of spinach, washed and trimmed with stems discarded

2 red or golden Delicious apples, cored and diced

2/3 cup dry roasted peanuts, coarsely chopped

1/2 cup raisins

1/2 cup green onions, thinly sliced

2 tablespoons sesame seeds, toasted

In a small jar, combine dressing ingredients and shake well. Let dressing stand 2 hours or more at room temperature to blend the flavors.

Tear the spinach into bite-size pieces. In a large salad bowl, combine all salad ingredients. Shake dressing well, add desired amount to salad and toss.

Serves 12.

Page sponsored by The Lafayette School District Governing Board
Chet Crabtree, Tom Hughes, Mary McCosker, Judy Miller, JoAnn Shogan

NY Deli Slaw

3/4 cup sugar
1/2 cup vinegar
1/2 cup vegetable oil
1 teaspoon salt
Dash of pepper
1/2 teaspoon celery seed
1 cabbage, shredded
1 large onion, finely chopped
1 green bell pepper, finely chopped
1 carrot, grated
Rings of red and yellow bell peppers

In a saucepan, bring the first 6 ingredients to a boil. Remove from the heat and let stand for 5 minutes. Combine cabbage, onion, green pepper and carrot. Pour dressing over mixture and stir. Cover and chill *overnight*. Drain excess dressing. Garnish with pepper rings and serve.

Serves 6-8.

Page sponsored by R. T. Steffens
TRI Commercial Real Estate Services, Walnut Creek 930-0930

Oriental Cabbage Salad

Salad
2 packages Ramen Noodles
2 1/2 cups shredded green cabbage*
1/2 cup shredded purple cabbage*
2 carrots, peeled and shredded
8 ounces canned water chestnuts, drained and chopped
1 cup chopped celery
1/2 cup almonds, sliced
1/2 cup sunflower seeds

Dressing
2 tablespoons vinegar
2 tablespoons sugar
3/4 cup vegetable oil
2 Ramen seasoning packets

Cook the Ramen noodles in boiling water and drain. Cool and add the cabbage, carrots, water chestnuts and celery. Mix the dressing ingredients and stir into the salad. Refrigerate. Add the almonds and sunflower seeds just before serving.

Serves 6.

*An 8 ounce package of coleslaw mix, available at well stocked markets, may be easily substituted.

Cucumber Salad

5 large cucumbers, peeled and
     very thinly sliced
Salt
2 cups sour cream
1 small onion, chopped
3 tablespoons cider vinegar
1 1/2 tablespoons sugar
Pepper
Paprika

Salt the cucumbers well. Place them in a strainer and top with a heavy bowl to weigh them down. This process causes excess moisture to be released. Drain for approximately 2 hours, stirring occasionally.

In a large bowl, mix the sour cream, onion, vinegar, sugar and pepper. Stir in the cucumbers. Chill. Before serving, dust with paprika.

Serves 8-10.

NOTE: This salad goes well with Vietnamese 5-Spice Chicken on page 80.

Page sponsored by J. Linneman & Co., San Francisco
John H. Linneman, John J. Mara, Eugene C. Phillips

Green Beans with Mustard Vinaigrette

1 pound green beans - trimmed

2 tablespoons Dijon mustard

Dash of lemon juice

3 tablespoons boiling water

1/4 cup olive oil

1/4 cup chopped fresh parsley

2 tablespoons chopped chives

Salt and pepper

Blanch the green beans in boiling, salted water for 3-5 minutes. Drain, cool and set aside. In a bowl, combine the mustard, lemon juice and water. Whisk in the oil and add the parsley and chives. Season with salt and pepper. Toss with the green beans. Cover and chill for several hours.

Serves 6-8.

Page sponsored by Kelly Tama Shiffman Inc.
Certified Public Accountants, Walnut Creek 933-0133

Greek Tomato Salad

5 tomatoes, chopped
2 tablespoons feta cheese, crumbled
5 green onions, chopped
1/2 tablespoon capers
1/2 cup olive oil
1/4 cup wine vinegar
1 teaspoon Dijon mustard
1 clove garlic, crushed

Combine the tomatoes, feta, onions and capers. In a separate bowl, whisk the remaining ingredients and add to the salad, stirring to combine.

Serves 3-4.

Page sponsored by Freddie's Pizza, Lafayette 284-9110
Donna Sohr and Gary Obrand

Basque Pickled Beans

1 pound dry garbanzo beans

1/2 cup chopped green onion

2 cloves garlic, crushed

1/2 cup chopped fresh parsley

3/4 cup red wine vinegar

1 1/4 cups vegetable oil

1 teaspoon salt

1/2 teaspoon fresh pepper, coarsely ground

1/4 teaspoon oregano

2 tablespoons chopped pimiento

In a 3-4 quart covered saucepan, soak the beans **overnight** in 8 cups of water. After soaking, drain and return the beans to the saucepan with 2 1/2 quarts of fresh water. Cook until tender, about 1 1/2 hours. Rinse well in cool water and drain.

While the beans are cooking make a marinade by combining the remaining ingredients. Pour the marinade over the warm beans. Stir well and chill at least 6 hours.

Page sponsored by J. Craig Smith, D. V. M., Moraga 376-1824

Russian Salad

Dressing

1 tablespoon mayonnaise

3 tablespoons sour cream

1 teaspoon lemon juice

1 teaspoon Dijon mustard

1 teaspoon dill

1/8 teaspoon paprika

Salt

Salad

1 cup peas

1 cup diced carrots

4 potatoes, chopped

1 cucumber, chopped

1 dill pickle, chopped

1 red apple, chopped

1/2 cup chopped mushrooms

1 head of lettuce

Blend all of the dressing ingredients.

Blanch the peas, carrots and potatoes until tender. Cool. Add the cucumber, pickle, apple and mushrooms. Combine with the dressing and chill.

Serve on a bed of lettuce.

Serves 4-6.

Page sponsored by Dawson Electric, Concord 686-3535

German Potato Salad

1/2 pound bacon

3/4 cup chopped onion

1 tablespoon flour

2 teaspoons salt

1/4 teaspoon freshly ground pepper

1 1/4 teaspoons sugar

1/2 cup cider vinegar

1/2 cup water

3 pounds russet potatoes, cooked,
   peeled and thinly sliced

1 1/2 teaspoons celery seeds

6 tablespoons chopped fresh parsley

Fry the bacon until crisp. Remove from the skillet, crumble and set aside.
Retain 6 tablespoons of bacon drippings. In the same pan, sauté the onions for
1 minute. Add the flour, salt, pepper and sugar. Stir in the vinegar and water.
Cook for 10 minutes.

Layer 1/3 of the potatoes in a casserole. Sprinkle with 1/3 of the celery seeds and
1/3 of the parsley. Continue with 1/3 of the bacon followed by 1/3 of the
vinegar mixture. Repeat to make 3 layers. Serve just warm or reheat in a
medium oven for 15 minutes.

Serves 8.

Page sponsored by Carolyn Way
John M. Grubb Realtors, Orinda 254-6033

Artichoke Rice Salad

1 package chicken flavor rice mix
6 ounces marinated artichoke hearts
8 ounces canned water chestnuts,
  drained and chopped
4 green onions, thinly sliced
1/3 cup mayonnaise
3 1/2 ounces slivered almonds

Cook the rice according to directions. Cool. Drain and slice the artichoke hearts, reserving 1/2 of the marinade. Combine the rice, water chestnuts, green onions, artichoke hearts and reserved marinade. Chill, *preferably overnight*. Just before serving, add the mayonnaise and almonds.

Serves 4.

Page sponsored by Derco Jewelers, San Francisco 626-7442

Confetti Rice Salad

Salad
10 ounces frozen chopped spinach, thawed
1 1/2 cups cooked long grain white or brown rice
1 cup chopped tomatoes
1/2 cup chopped green onions
1/2 cup chopped celery
2 tablespoons unsalted sunflower seeds

Dressing
2 tablespoons tarragon vinegar
2 tablespoons olive oil
1 teaspoon dill weed
3/4 teaspoon dry mustard
Pepper

Squeeze the liquid from the spinach. Mix the salad ingredients in a medium bowl. Combine the dressing ingredients in a blender or food processor. Toss the salad with the dressing. Chill until ready to serve.

Serves 6.

Page sponsored by Crowder Construction, Alamo 820-5599

Tortellini Salad

1/3 cup olive oil

1/2 cup finely chopped fresh parsley

2 tablespoons vinegar

1/3 cup chopped fresh basil

1/3 cup chopped red onion

2 cloves garlic, crushed

1/2 teaspoon pepper

Pinch of nutmeg

8 ounces feta or farmers cheese,
   cut into 1/2" cubes

1 pound fresh tortellini, cooked al dente

1/4 pound salami, cut into strips

1 cup pitted ripe olives, quartered

2 tomatoes, diced

1/2 bell pepper, sliced

In a jar, combine the first 8 ingredients. Shake well. Combine the remaining ingredients in a medium bowl. Add the dressing and toss.

Serves 6.

Page sponsored by Katherine Jernberg and Stephen Stanley

Cilantro Chicken Salad

1/4 cup olive oil
1/4 cup vegetable oil
4 tablespoons red wine vinegar
1 teaspoon dry marjoram
1/4 teaspoon salt
1/4 cup finely chopped fresh cilantro
15 ounces garbanzos, drained
1 small red onion, thinly sliced
3 ounces pitted ripe olives, drained
4 chicken breast halves
1 bunch fresh spinach or mixed greens
Cherry tomatoes, halved

Combine the first 6 ingredients to make a marinade. Add the garbanzos, onions and olives to the marinade. Stir gently to mix. Cover and refrigerate **overnight.**

Cook, skin, bone and thinly slice the chicken.

Tear the greens into bite-size pieces and arrange on individual serving plates. To serve, fold the chicken into the marinade and spoon on top of the bed of greens.

Garnish with tomatoes.

Page sponsored by Dr. Richard Mollberg, Podiatrist, Concord 827-4056

Curry Salad

Salad
6 cups shredded lettuce
1/4 pound bean sprouts
8 ounces canned sliced water chestnuts
1/2 cup thinly sliced green onions
1 cucumber, peeled and thinly sliced
4 cups cooked chicken cut into strips
12 ounces sugar snap peas
1/2 cup slivered almonds
18 cherry tomatoes

Dressing
2 cups mayonnaise
2 teaspoons curry powder
1 teaspoon sugar
1/2 teaspoon ginger
Salt and pepper

In a 4 quart dish, layer lettuce, sprouts, water chestnuts, green onions, cucumbers, chicken and peas.

Combine all of the dressing ingredients. Pour the dressing over the salad to cover. Seal with plastic wrap and refrigerate **overnight**.

To serve, top with slivered almonds and cherry tomatoes.

Serves 8-10.

Page sponsored by Dorothy June and Danny Neblett
In honor of Danielle & Sacha Silvani and Sophia & Susannah Maund

Chinese Chicken Salad

Salad

3 chicken breast halves

1 head lettuce, shredded

5 ounces crispy chow mein noodles

4 green onions, sliced

Dressing

2 tablespoons toasted sesame seeds

1 teaspoon salt

1/2 teaspoon pepper

1/3 cup olive oil

2 cloves garlic, minced

3 tablespoons vinegar

2 tablespoons chopped peanuts

2 tablespoons sugar

Cook, skin, bone and shred the chicken.

Combine the chicken, lettuce, noodles and green onions. Combine the dressing ingredients and mix well. Pour over the salad and toss.

Serves 8-10.

Page sponsored by the Springhill Elementary School Staff
In memory of Mary McIvor

Tokyo Chicken's Salad Dressing
From Tokyo Chicken Restaurant, Lafayette

1 cup white miso (bean paste)
1 cup sugar
1/3 cup sweet sake (mirin)
1 1/2 teaspoons sesame seed oil
2 cups rice vinegar
4 cups apple juice

In a large saucepan, mix all ingredients except the apple juice. Bring to a boil, stirring until the sugar is dissolved. Blend in the apple juice.

Cool and refrigerate.

Celery Seed Dressing

2/3 cup sugar
1/2 teaspoon dry mustard
1 teaspoon salt
1/2 cup cider vinegar
1 cup vegetable oil
1 tablespoon celery seeds
1 small onion, finely grated

With an electric beater, blend the sugar, mustard and salt. Add the vinegar and blend on medium speed. Slowly add the oil and continue beating for 10 minutes. Add the celery seeds and grated onion. Stir to blend.

NOTE: This dressing is very good on a fresh fruit salad. It keeps well in the refrigerator for months in a tightly covered container.

Blue Cheese Dressing

4 ounces crumbled blue cheese
1 1/3 cups sour cream
1 teaspoon salt
2 teaspoons Worcestershire sauce
1/2 teaspoon dry onion flakes
Dash of Tabasco sauce
1/2 cup cider vinegar
1 1/2 cups mayonnaise

Combine all ingredients and chill.

Makes 1 quart of dressing.

Dilled Louis Dressing

1/4 cup ketchup

1/4 cup chili sauce

1/2 green bell pepper, cut into 1" pieces

2 green onions, cut into 1" pieces

1/2 clove garlic, coarsely chopped

2-3 sprigs fresh parsley

1 cup mayonnaise

1 hard boiled egg, coarsely chopped

4 sweet pickles, coarsely chopped

1/2 teaspoon dill weed

Salt and pepper

Blend the first 6 ingredients in a food processor or blender until smooth. Add the mayonnaise and blend. Pour the mixture into a bowl and stir in the eggs, pickles, dill, salt and pepper. Chill.

NOTE: This dressing is wonderful on green or seafood salads.

Page sponsored by Michael J. Sayegh, D.D.S., Lafayette 284-4744

Green Goddess Dressing

5 green onions, cut into 1" lengths
3 cloves garlic, peeled and coarsely chopped
2 tablespoons lemon juice
1/4 cup red wine vinegar
2 ounces anchovy fillets, drained
1 cup sour cream
2 tablespoons curry powder
1/3 cup prepared yellow mustard
1 bunch parsley
3 cups mayonnaise

Blend the first 8 ingredients in a food processor or blender. Add the parsley and blend thoroughly. Add the mayonnaise and blend again.

Makes 2 cups of dressing.

Page sponsored by Morehouse Foods, Inc., Emeryville

ENTREES

Roast Pork with Sausage Stuffing
Barbecued Pork Loin
Burgundy Braised Ham
Country Spareribs
Barbecued Spareribs
Chili Verde
Calcutta Curry
Butterflied Leg of Lamb
Roasted Leg of Lamb
Pbulgogi - Barbecued Korean Beef
Teriyaki Flank Steak
Beef Zinfandel
Mediterranean Beef Stew
Sauerbraten
Lillyan's Luxembourg Chili
Lentil Chili
Cattlemen's Chili
Lasagne with Bolognese Sauce
Baked Cilantro Chicken
Chicken Piri Piri
Chicken Fricassee with Dumplings
Swiss Chicken Pie
Vietnamese Five Spice Chicken
Grilled Herb Chicken
Chicken Sauté with Curry and Basil
Pesto Chicken
Sonoma Chicken
Poulet en Vin Blanc

Petti Di Polla
Prime Thyme Chicken
Renaissance Chicken
Polenta Strata
Maple Roast Turkey with Corn Bread Stuffing
Curried Turkey Croissant with Cranberry Chutney
Brown Rice Jambalaya
Cioppino
Kona Coast Mahi Mahi
Fresh Catch
Connecticut Scallops and Shrimp
Scampi
Mussels inWhite Wine
Marinades
Fish Sauce Medley
Pacific Coast Pasta
Linguine with Clam Sauce
Pasta Puttanesca
Penne with Swiss Chard
Lasagne with Tomato Herb Sauce
Elizabeth's Chili Relleno Casserole
Vegetarian Burritos with Peanut Sauce

Roast Pork with Sausage Stuffing

Roast

1 teaspoon pepper

2 teaspoons salt

1 1/2 teaspoons thyme

2 teaspoons sage

8 pound (16 rib) crown roast of pork

Vegetable oil

Sausage Stuffing

1 1/2 cups wild rice, rinsed and drained

2 teaspoons fennel seeds

3 cups chicken broth

4 tablespoons unsalted butter

1 pound sweet Italian sausage, casings removed

2 cups chopped onion

3 small fennel bulbs, chopped
    (approximately 3 cups)

Combine the seasonings and rub over pork roast. Chill, covered, **overnight.**

Preheat oven to 450° F.

In a large saucepan, combine the rice, fennel seeds, chicken broth and
2 tablespoons of the butter. Bring to a boil and simmer, partially covered, for
45 to 55 minutes. Drain any excess liquid.

In a skillet, cook the sausage and drain. Finely grind the sausage and set aside.
In the same skillet, melt the remaining butter and cook the onion until soft.
Add the fennel and cook an additional 5 minutes until tender. Combine the
rice, sausage and fennel mixture to complete the stuffing.

Pat the roast with vegetable oil. Lightly oil the roasting pan. Set the pork in
the pan and mound the stuffing in the middle of the crown. Cover with a lightly
oiled round of foil. Roast for 20 minutes. Lower the heat to 325° F. and
continue roasting for 1 3/4 hours or until meat thermometer registers 160° F.
Remove from the oven and let stand for 10 minutes before slicing into
individual chops.

Serves 12.

Barbecued Pork Loin

3 tablespoons rock salt
1 teaspoon freshly ground pepper
1 teaspoon thyme
1 tablespoon rosemary
1/4 teaspoon allspice
4 cloves garlic, minced
3/4 cup brandy or vermouth
1 pork loin roast, butterflied

Combine all ingredients, except the roast, in a glass dish. Place the pork in the marinade and turn to coat. Marinate in the refrigerator **overnight** or for at least 8 hours.

Using the indirect heat method, barbecue the roast for about 17 minutes per pound. Slice and serve.

Serves 6-8.

Page sponsored by Longs Drug Stores, Contra Costa County

Burgundy Braised Ham

1/4 pound carrots, peeled and sliced
1/4 pound onions, sliced
2 tablespoons butter
1 tablespoon vegetable oil
8-10 pound ham, trimmed of excess fat
6 parsley sprigs
1 bay leaf
6 peppercorns
1/2 teaspoon thyme
3 whole cloves
4 cups white burgundy wine
4-6 cups chicken or beef stock

Preheat oven to 325° F.

In a roasting pan or fireproof casserole large enough to hold the ham, sauté the vegetables in butter and oil until tender and lightly browned. Place the ham over the vegetables, fatty side up. Combine the remaining ingredients and pour over the ham. Bring to a simmer on the stovetop. Cover and bake approximately 2 hours, basting every 20 minutes. Roast until the thickest part of the meat can be easily pierced. Remove ham, slice and serve.

Country Spareribs

5 pounds baby back pork ribs or
   country style spareribs
1 piece ginger, 2-3 inches long,
   peeled and crushed
5 cloves garlic, crushed
1 cup sugar
1 cup ketchup
3/4 cup soy sauce
1/3 cup oyster sauce

Cut the ribs into 2-3 rib sections. Place them in a large stock pot with the ginger and garlic. Fill with cold water. Cover the pot and bring to a boil. Simmer for 45 minutes. Combine the remaining ingredients in a bowl. Drain the spareribs and marinate them in the sauce for a few hours. When ready to serve, broil or barbecue about 5-10 minutes on each side. To serve, cut into single rib pieces.

Serves 6.

Barbecued Spareribs

Ribs
4 pounds pork spareribs
1 onion, quartered
2 teaspoons salt
1/4 teaspoon pepper

Sauce
1/2 cup cider vinegar
1/2 cup ketchup
1/4 cup chili sauce
1/4 cup Worcestershire sauce
2 tablespoons chopped onion
1 tablespoon lemon juice
1/2 cup light brown sugar
1/2 teaspoon dry mustard
1 clove garlic, crushed
Dash of cayenne pepper

In a large kettle, place the ribs, onion, salt, pepper and cover with 3 quarts of water. Bring to a boil. Reduce the heat, cover and simmer for 1 1/2 hours or until tender. Drain.

While the ribs are cooking, in a medium saucepan, combine all of the sauce ingredients. Simmer uncovered for 1 hour, stirring occasionally.

Arrange the spareribs on the grill and brush with sauce. Barbecue 10 minutes on each side basting frequently. These can also be done under a broiler, 5 inches from the heat.

Serves 4-6.

Chili Verde

1 tablespoon vegetable oil

2 pounds pork, diced

14 ounces canned Ortega green chili salsa

8 ounces canned green chilies, diced

Diced jalapeños, to taste

2 stalks celery, chopped

1/2 onion, chopped

2 tomatoes, chopped

Garlic salt

Flour tortillas

Grated cheese

Sour cream

Guacamole

In a lightly oiled frying pan, cook the pork over medium heat until it is no longer pink. Add the salsa, chilies, jalapeños, celery, onion, tomatoes and garlic salt. Cover and simmer for about 30 minutes. Serve as a burrito filling inside warm flour tortillas, garnished with grated cheese, sour cream and guacamole.

Page sponsored by Hickey & Hill, Inc.
Turnaround Managers and Consultants, Lafayette 283-7802

Calcutta Curry

2 tablespoons butter
2 pounds lamb shoulder,
    cut into 3/4" cubes
1 onion, chopped
1 stalk celery, chopped
1 Pippin apple, cored and chopped
1 tablespoon curry powder
1 bay leaf
1/4 cup dry white wine
1 cup chicken broth
1 cup coconut milk
Juice of half a lime
1/2 cup sour cream
Steamed rice

Suggested Condiments
Chutney
Raisins
Salted peanuts
Shredded coconut
Sliced green onions
Diced cucumber
Diced banana

In a skillet, melt the butter and brown the lamb cubes quickly. Remove and set aside. In the same skillet, sauté the onion, celery and apple until onion is soft. Add the curry powder and bay leaf, and cook 2 minutes longer. Add the wine and stir to deglaze the pan. Stir in chicken stock and add the lamb. Cover and simmer for 1 hour.

NOTE: At this point the curry may be refrigerated for up to 2 days.

30 minutes before serving, stir in the coconut milk and lime juice. Cook over low heat until the curry is thickened. Just before serving, remove from the heat and stir in the sour cream. Serve over steamed white rice with your choice of condiments.

NOTE: Naan, the Indian yogurt bread on page 145 goes well with this curry.

Page sponsored by The Andron Family

Butterflied Leg of Lamb

1 leg of lamb, boned and butterflied
1 onion, sliced
1 clove garlic, minced
Juice of one lemon
1/2 cup cider vinegar or dry red wine
1/4 teaspoon oregano
1/4 teaspoon thyme
1/2 teaspoon rosemary
1/2 teaspoon basil
1 teaspoon salt
1/8 teaspoon pepper

In a shallow glass baking dish, place the flattened lamb, topping it with onion slices. Combine the remaining ingredients in a small bowl and pour over the lamb. Marinate for several hours in the refrigerator turning occasionally.

With the fat side down, grill over hot coals, basting occasionally with the marinade. Turn and grill until the lamb is cooked through. Slice and serve.

Serves 6-8.

Page sponsored by Chinn Workshops and S.A.T. Preparation, Lafayette 283-8443

Roasted Leg of Lamb

Lamb
1 leg of lamb
5 slices fresh ginger
5 cloves garlic
2 teaspoons fresh rosemary
Olive oil
1/2 cup Gulden's mustard
Salt and pepper
1 onion, quartered
1 carrot, diced

Gravy
Roasted lamb drippings
4 tablespoons butter, melted
3 tablespoons flour
1 cup beef broth
1 shallot, chopped
1 tablespoon chopped fresh ginger
Salt and pepper

Preheat oven to 375º F.

Make 5 slits in the fat side of the lamb. In each slit, place a piece of ginger, a clove of garlic, and a sprig of rosemary. In a large frying pan, brown the lamb in oil over high heat.

Spread the lamb with mustard. Place it in a roasting pan, fat side up and sprinkle with salt and pepper. Place the onion and carrot in the pan around the roast. Cover with foil and roast for approximately 1 1/4 hours or until done. Remove the lamb and tent with the foil to keep warm. Drain excess grease, reserving drippings in the roasting pan for the gravy.

Place the roasting pan over low heat and add the butter, scraping with a spatula to loosen drippings. Sprinkle in the flour and stir to form a roux. Slowly add beef broth, stirring constantly to blend the ingredients. Add the shallots, ginger, salt and pepper. Cook to desired thickness. Slice the lamb and serve with gravy.

Serves 8.

Pbulgogi
Barbecued Korean Beef

2 pounds sirloin tip beef,
   sliced thinly against the grain
8 tablespoons soy sauce
2 tablespoons vegetable oil
2 tablespoons Oriental sesame oil
3 tablespoons brown sugar
2 teaspoons garlic, minced
2 slices fresh ginger, minced
1 green onion, chopped
Dash of black pepper

Soak bamboo skewers in water at least 1 hour. This will prevent them from splintering and burning on the grill.

Weave the beef on bamboo skewers. Mix the remaining ingredients in a 9" x 13" glass dish making sure the brown sugar is completely dissolved. Add skewered beef, turning to coat. Marinate 2-3 hours, turning occasionally. Barbecue quickly over hot coals.

Serves 4.

———————— ❧ ————————

Teriyaki Flank Steak

2 pounds flank steak
1/2 cup soy sauce
1/2 cup water
3 tablespoons lemon juice
4 heaping tablespoons brown sugar
2 cloves garlic, minced
2 slices fresh ginger, minced
Freshly ground pepper

Place beef in a shallow glass dish. Combine the remaining ingredients in a small bowl, stirring until the sugar dissolves. Pour over the meat, turning to coat. Marinate in the refrigerator at least 3 hours, turning occasionally. Barbecue or broil.

Serves 4.

Page sponsored by the Lafayette Education Association, Lafayette School District

Beef Zinfandel

3 slices bacon, minced
1/4 cup vegetable oil
1/2 red onion, chopped
1 clove garlic, minced
1 1/2 pounds lean beef, cut into 1" cubes
1/3 cup flour
2 teaspoons Lawry's seasoned salt
1/4 teaspoon pepper
1/4 cup brandy
1 cup beef broth
1 cup red Zinfandel wine
1 bay leaf
2 carrots, peeled and cut into 1" slices
2 potatoes, peeled and cut into 1" pieces
6 mushrooms, quartered

Cook bacon in a Dutch oven until crisp. Remove and set aside. Add the oil, onion and garlic to the bacon drippings. Coat the meat with flour, seasoned salt and pepper, and brown.

In a small saucepan, heat the brandy and set aflame. Pour over the meat and add the broth, wine and bay leaf. Bring to a boil, reduce heat, cover and simmer for 1 hour. Add the carrots and potatoes. Cover and cook for 20 minutes. Add the mushrooms and cook for 10 minutes. Remove the bay leaf and stir in reserved bacon.

Serves 4.

Mediterranean Beef Stew

2 cups flour
1 1/2 tablespoons thyme
1/2 teaspoon salt
1/2 teaspoon pepper
3 pounds lean stew meat, cut into 1" cubes
1/4 cup vegetable oil
1 cup red wine
1 cup crushed tomatoes
1 1/2 cups beef stock
2 tablespoons cumin
1 1/2 teaspoons chili powder
1 bay leaf
Salt and pepper
12 pearl onions, peeled
8 cloves garlic, minced
3/4 cup chopped parsley
1 cup Italian green olives

Stir together flour, thyme, salt and pepper. Coat the meat with flour mixture, shaking off excess. In a large stew pot, heat the oil. Add the beef and brown on all sides. Transfer to paper towels to drain. To the pot, add wine, tomatoes and beef stock. Bring to a boil over medium heat. Return the beef to the pot, add the cumin, chili powder, bay leaf, salt and pepper to taste. Cover the pot and simmer 1 hour. Add the onions and simmer uncovered for 15 minutes. Add the garlic, parsley, olives and simmer until thickened, about 10 minutes.

Serves 6 - 8.

Page sponsored by Luciani-Schlatter & Associates, San Francisco

Sauerbraten

Marinade	Beef
1 cup water	2 pounds chuck roast
1 cup wine vinegar	2 tablespoons flour
1 onion, chopped	1/2 cup vegetable oil
1 carrot, peeled and chopped	1/4 cup bacon drippings
1 tomato, chopped	Salt
4 cloves	1 cup water
4 juniper berries	1/2 cup red wine
1 celery root, chopped	2 tablespoons heavy cream

In a saucepan, combine all the marinade ingredients and boil for 20 minutes. Let cool. Place the meat in the marinade and refrigerate for **4 days, turning occasionally.**

Remove the meat, dust with flour and sprinkle with salt. In a Dutch oven, heat the oil and bacon drippings. Brown the meat. Remove the vegetables from the marinade and add to the meat. Add the water and wine and simmer for 3 hours, adding more water if necessary.

Make the gravy using the beef drippings and 4 tablespoons of the marinade. Simmer for 2 minutes. Add the cream, heat through, and serve over noodles.

Serves 6.

Lillyan's Luxembourg Chili
From John A. Brown Kitchenwares, Oakland

1 pound ground beef
1 tablespoon vegetable oil
2 onions, chopped
1/2 cup chopped green pepper
12 ounces canned tomatoes
8 ounces tomato sauce
15 ounces tomato purée
2 bay leaves
Salt and pepper
1 tablespoon chili powder
15 ounces canned red kidney beans

In a large sauté pan or 3 quart saucepan, brown the ground beef in oil. Add all remaining ingredients except the beans. Simmer 1 1/2 hours or longer if thicker chili is preferred. Add the beans, heat through and serve hot.

Serves 4-6.

Lentil Chili

1 pound dry lentils, rinsed

1 pound lean ground beef

2 tablespoons vegetable oil

1 onion, chopped

2 cloves garlic, minced

2 tablespoons chili powder

16 ounces tomato sauce

Salt

Cayenne pepper

In a 5 quart stock pot, cook the lentils in 2 quarts of boiling, salted water until tender, approximately 30 minutes. Drain and set lentils aside.

In the same stock pot, cook the ground beef over medium heat until browned and crumbly. Add the oil, onion and garlic. Sauté until the onion is limp. Add the chili powder and tomato sauce. Simmer, covered for 15 minutes. Add the lentils and simmer until heated through. Add salt and cayenne pepper. Thin with water to desired consistency.

Serves 6.

NOTE: This chili is delicious served with a variety of condiments such as tortilla chips, shredded lettuce, diced green pepper, chopped red onion, shredded Jack or cheddar cheese, diced avocado or salsa.

Page sponsored by Pilgrim Fireplace Equipment
American Made Fireplace Accessories, Richmond 529-2050

Cattlemen's Chili

2 pounds round or chuck steak, cut into 1/4" cubes
2 tablespoons olive oil
2 pounds ground beef
2 onions, chopped
10 garlic cloves, coarsely chopped
1 pound chorizo
16 ounces tomato sauce
4 tablespoons Grandma's chili powder, or to taste
1 tablespoon cumin
2 teaspoons oregano
1 teaspoon salt
1/2 teaspoon cayenne pepper
24 ounces beer
32 ounces kidney beans, drained
4 ounces canned chopped green chiles
Sour cream

In a large frying pan, brown the steak and ground beef in the oil. Add the onions and garlic and cook for 5 minutes. Drain well. Fry the chorizo separately and drain.

In a large saucepan, combine all ingredients. Cook over low heat for 1 1/2 - 2 hours, until the steak is tender. Serve in chili bowls with a dollop of sour cream.

Serves 10.

Lasagne with Bolognese Sauce

Lasagne

Bolognese sauce (recipe included)
16 ounces lasagne noodles, cooked al dente
2 pounds mozzarella cheese, grated
1 pound ricotta cheese
6 ounces parmesan cheese, grated

Bolognese Sauce

2 pounds ground beef
1 pound Italian sausage with fennel,
   casings removed
3 cups chopped onion
6 cloves garlic, minced
1 tablespoon salt
32 ounces tomato sauce
32 ounces whole tomatoes
6 ounces tomato paste
1 tablespoon Worcestershire sauce
1 tablespoon red wine vinegar
1 teaspoon Tabasco sauce

1 teaspoon basil
1 teaspoon rosemary
1 teaspoon marjoram
2 tablespoons oregano
1 tablespoon chili powder
1 tablespoon paprika
1 tablespoon sugar
1 teaspoon pepper
3 bay leaves
3 cups minced green bell pepper
1 cup fresh parsley, minced
2 cups sliced mushrooms

Bolognese Sauce: In a large, heavy frying pan, brown the meats, onion and garlic with salt, stirring frequently. Drain and set aside.

In a large heavy pot, combine the remaining ingredients and the meat. Stir well and bring to a boil. Reduce heat, cover and simmer slowly for 5-6 hours.

Preheat oven to 350º F.

Lasagne: In a deep 9" x 13" casserole, layer sauce, noodles, sauce, mozzarella and ricotta cheeses. Repeat. Top with sauce and lots of grated mozzarella. Sprinkle parmesan evenly over the entire top.

Cover loosely with foil and bake for 45 minutes. Uncover and continue baking until the top is lightly browned and lasagne is bubbly.

NOTE: This lasagne may be made with sheets of fresh pasta. If done this way, there is no need to cook the pasta before assembling the lasagne, but be sure to leave enough room in the pan for the pasta to expand. The leftover sauce freezes well and may be used as a sauce over any type of pasta.

Baked Cilantro Chicken

1 large chicken
1 bunch fresh cilantro
4 cloves garlic, sliced
8 1/8" slices fresh ginger, peeled
2 limes, halved
2 tablespoons soy sauce
1 teaspoon Oriental sesame oil
Several drops hot chili oil
1/2 onion, quartered

Preheat oven to 325° F.

Remove excess fat from the chicken cavity. Gently work your fingers between the skin and breast meat to create a space. Insert several small bunches of cilantro. Cut a small slit between each breast and leg. Stuff each slit with 1 slice of garlic and 1 slice of ginger. Squeeze lime juice over the entire chicken, reserving the peels.

In a small bowl, mix the soy sauce, sesame oil, hot chili oil and baste the entire chicken. Stuff the cavity with alternating layers of onion, lime peels, remaining cilantro, garlic and ginger slices. In a glass baking dish, bake for 1 1/2 hours uncovered.

Serves 4.

—————————— 🌶 ——————————

Chicken Piri Piri

1 tablespoon ground piri piri*
3 garlic cloves, chopped
1 cup peanut or vegetable oil
1/4 cup fresh lemon juice
1 teaspoon salt
3 pound chicken

Combine the piri piri, garlic and 1/2 cup oil in a food processor or blender. Pour the mixture into a glass dish. Stir in remaining oil, lemon juice and salt. Add the chicken and marinate for 2 hours at room temperature or **overnight** in the refrigerator turning occasionally. Barbecue using indirect heat for 1 1/2 hours.

Serves 4.

*Piri piri is available at specialty food stores. 1-2 tablespoons of red pepper flakes may be substituted.

Page sponsored by KRT Marketing, Lafayette 284-0444
In honor of the Lafayette Community's support of education

Chicken Fricassee with Dumplings

Chicken

5-6 pounds chicken parts, seasoned with salt & pepper
1/2 cup butter
2 tablespoons vegetable oil
7 cups chicken broth
1 onion, stuck with 2 cloves
1 carrot, halved
2 celery tops
1 bay leaf
2 sprigs of parsley
1/2 cup flour
1/2 cup heavy cream
Salt and pepper

Dumplings

2 cups flour
4 teaspoons baking powder
1 1/2 teaspoons salt
1/4 cup shortening
2 eggs, lightly beaten
2/3 cup milk
1/4 cup minced fresh parsley

Chicken: In a large skillet, sauté the chicken in 1/4 cup butter and 2 tablespoons oil until well browned. Transfer it to a large kettle and add the broth, onion, carrot, celery, bay leaf and parsley. Bring to a boil, skimming off the froth as it rises to the surface. Reduce the heat and simmer, covered for 1 1/4 hours until chicken is very tender. Transfer the chicken to a platter and keep it warm.

Skim the fat from the stock, strain it through a sieve and reserve 4 cups.

Page sponsored by The Dudum's - Jim, Denise, Jason, Keith, Daryl and J.D.

In a large flame-proof casserole, melt the remaining butter. Add the flour to form a roux and cook over low heat for 3 minutes, stirring constantly. Remove the casserole from the heat and in a steady stream, add the reserved stock, stirring constantly. Bring to a boil, reduce the heat and simmer for 10 minutes. Add the cream, salt and pepper to taste. Add the chicken and simmer over low heat while preparing the dumplings.

Dumplings: Combine the flour, baking powder and salt. Cut in the shortening until the mixture resembles corn meal.

Mix the eggs, milk and parsley, and add to the flour mixture. Stir until the flour is just moistened.

Drop by tablespoonfuls onto simmering chicken fricassee. Cover to steam dumplings for 12 minutes.

Serves 6-8.

Swiss Chicken Pie

Chicken
3 - 4 pound chicken
1 carrot, cut in half
2 stalks celery, cut in half
1 onion, cut in half
1 bay leaf
Water

Filling
1/4 cup chopped celery
1/4 cup frozen petite peas
1/4 cup chopped carrots
1 tablespoon chopped onion
3 tablespoons flour
3 tablespoons dry bread crumbs
1/4 teaspoon sage
1/2 teaspoon thyme
1 tablespoon chopped fresh parsley
1/2 teaspoon coarsely ground pepper
1/2 teaspoon salt
1/2 cup reserved chicken stock

Crust
3 cups flour
1 1/4 cups vegetable shortening
1 1/2 teaspoons salt
2 tablespoons sugar
1/4 cup milk
1/4 cup water
2 tablespoons butter
1 egg yolk, beaten

To Serve
Dijon mustard
Swiss cheese, thinly sliced

Chicken: Remove giblets, neck, etc., from inside the cavity of the chicken. Place the chicken in a dutch oven with the carrot, celery, onion and bay leaf. Fill the dutch oven half way with water. Bring to a boil, reduce heat, cover and simmer for 45 minutes. Remove the chicken, discard vegetables and reserve 1/2 cup of the chicken stock. This may be done one day ahead and refrigerated **overnight.** After chicken has cooled, remove skin and bones. Tear the meat into large pieces.

Page sponsored by Rex, Jane, Amalia and Bill Scatena

Filling: Place the torn chicken pieces in a large bowl. Add all the filling ingredients except chicken stock and toss. Add the chicken stock and blend. Set aside.

Preheat oven to 425°F.

Crust: Cut the shortening into the flour, salt and sugar until particles are the size of small peas. Blend in the milk and water to form a soft dough.

Divide the dough into two balls. Using a rolling pin, roll one ball out to fit into an 8" metal pie pan. Fill with chicken mixture and dot with butter. Roll out remaining dough and fit on top of the filling. Trim excess pastry and crimp around outer edge of pie. Brush the top of the pie with egg yolk.

Cover the crimped edge of the pie with 3" foil strips. Bake the pie for 15 minutes. Remove foil strips. Bake for an additional 25 minutes or until the crust is a deep golden brown. Let the pie set for 1 hour at room temperature. Pie may be made one day ahead. Before serving, bring it to room temperature.

To serve: Preheat oven to 400° F.

Cut the pie into serving slices and remove to individual ovenproof plates. Top each slice with Dijon mustard and a thin slice of Swiss cheese. Return to oven for 5 - 8 minutes or until the cheese melts.

Serves 6 - 8.

Vietnamese Five Spice Chicken

4 garlic cloves

2 shallots

1 1/2 tablespoons sugar

1 1/2 tablespoons soy sauce

1 1/2 tablespoons dry sherry

1/2 teaspoon salt

1/4 teaspoon pepper

1/2 teaspoon five spice powder

1 1/2 tablespoons Nuoc mam*

1 chicken, cut up

In a food processor or by hand, mince together garlic, shallots and sugar. Add the remaining ingredients except the chicken and mix thoroughly. Pour over the chicken and marinate in the refrigerator at least 4 hours or **overnight**. Barbecue or broil 15 minutes on each side. In a saucepan, simmer remaining marinade for 3-5 minutes. Pour over chicken and serve.

*Vietnamese fish sauce is available at well stocked specialty markets.

Serves 4-6.

Grilled Herb Chicken

4 chicken breasts, halved, skinned and boned
1/2 cup olive oil
1/2 cup freshly squeezed lemon juice
1 teaspoon Dijon mustard
4 cloves garlic, crushed
1/4 cup chopped fresh parsley
1 tablespoon chopped fresh rosemary
1 tablespoon chopped fresh sage
1 tablespoon chopped fresh tarragon
1 tablespoon chopped fresh oregano
1 tablespoon chopped fresh chives
1/2 teaspoon salt
Freshly ground pepper

Place chicken breasts in a marinating dish. Combine the remaining ingredients. Pour over the chicken and allow to marinate at least 2 hours.

Drain chicken, reserving the marinade. Grill the chicken breasts, brushing frequently with the marinade while cooking.

Serves 6.

Chicken Sauté with Curry and Basil

2 large chicken breasts,
   halved, skinned and boned
Salt and pepper
2 tablespoons butter
1 clove garlic, chopped
1/3 cup heavy cream
2 tablespoons water
1 1/2 teaspoons curry powder
1/2 cup lightly packed fresh
   basil leaves, shredded
Salt and pepper

Suggested Condiments
Chutney
Raisins
Salted peanuts
Shredded coconut
Sliced green onions
Diced cucumber
Diced bananas

Season the chicken with salt and pepper. In a large frying pan, melt the butter over medium heat. Brown the chicken until golden, turning once. Add chopped garlic and continue cooking for 30 seconds. Stir in 1/4 of the cream and 2 tablespoons of water. Reduce the heat to medium, cover and simmer until chicken is cooked through, approximately 5-8 minutes. Transfer chicken to a serving platter and keep warm.

Whisk in the remaining cream and curry powder, and simmer. Add the basil leaves. Season with salt and pepper as desired. Pour the sauce over the chicken and serve with rice and condiments.

Page sponsored by Athens Benefits Insurance Services, Concord 798-2780
Robert Torrey, President

Pesto Chicken

Pesto
1 cup fresh basil leaves
1/2 cup olive oil
1 tablespoon pine nuts
1/3 cup grated parmesan cheese
1/2 teaspoon salt

Chicken
2 whole chicken breasts,
   skinned and boned
6-8 slices prosciutto
5-6 tablespoons pesto
2/3 cup ricotta cheese
1/3 cup pine nuts
3 tablespoons olive oil
2 tablespoons butter
Salt and pepper
1 1/2 cups white wine

Preheat oven to 375° F.

Combine all pesto ingredients in a blender or food processor. Process and set aside.

Lay chicken breasts flat and pound, if desired. Place prosciutto slices on top. In a small bowl combine pesto, ricotta and pine nuts. Spread on prosciutto. Roll up chicken breasts and secure with toothpicks. Place in a baking dish, seam side down. Rub chicken with olive oil and dot with butter. Sprinkle with salt and pepper. Pour wine over chicken and bake 25 minutes.

Serves 4.

Page sponsored by The Layng Family

Sonoma Chicken

2 green onions, greens only

1/4 cup cream cheese, softened

1 tablespoon butter, softened

1 tablespoon sharp white cheddar cheese

2 teaspoons dry sherry

Pinch of nutmeg

1/8 cup grated Swiss cheese

4 whole chicken breasts, skinned and boned

2 1/2 tablespoons Dijon mustard

1 egg

1 cup milk

1 cup flour

1 cup bread crumbs

2 tablespoons olive oil

2 tablespoons butter

In a food processor, finely chop the green onions. Add the cream cheese, butter and cheddar cheese. Process until smooth. Add sherry and nutmeg and process until completely mixed. Place in the refrigerator to chill. When firm, divide into four portions and shape each into a cylindrical roll. Roll each in Swiss cheese to coat.

Place the chicken breasts between two sheets of wax paper and pound until thin. Spread one side with Dijon mustard and place one cheese roll in the middle of each chicken breast. Roll the chicken breast around the cheese making sure the cheese is completely covered. Whisk egg and milk together. Roll chicken breasts in the flour, then in the egg mixture, then in the bread crumbs. Refrigerate until chicken breasts are cold.

Preheat oven to 350º F.

Sauté the chicken breasts in oil and butter until golden on all sides. Place in a 9" square baking dish and bake 20-25 minutes until the chicken is tender yet firm to the touch.

Serves 4.

Poulet en Vin Blanc

8 tablespoons flour
Salt and pepper
Garlic salt
5 chicken breasts, halved,
   skinned and boned
12 tablespoons butter
2 1/2 cups chicken broth
1 cup white wine
4 green onions, sliced
1/2 pound mushrooms, sliced

Preheat oven to 350º F.

Combine 4 tablespoons of flour with the salt, pepper and garlic salt. Dust the chicken with the seasoned flour. Melt 8 tablespoons of butter in a shallow baking dish. Add the chicken, turning to coat and bake for 45 minutes or until tender.

In a frying pan, melt 4 tablespoons of butter. Slowly stir in the remaining flour to make a roux and cook for 1 minute. Add the chicken broth and wine, stirring constantly, until thickened and smooth.

When the chicken is done, turn the pieces over and cover with sauce. Sprinkle with the green onions and mushrooms. Reduce heat to 325º F. and bake 30 minutes.

Serves 8-10.

Page sponsored by Staglin Family Vineyard, Lafayette 284-5827

Petti Di Polla

4 chicken breasts, halved,
  skinned and boned
Seasoned salt
1/2 cup butter, softened
1/2 teaspoon oregano
1/2 teaspoon marjoram

1/2 teaspoon parsley
1/4 pound Monterey Jack cheese,
  sliced into 8 pieces
1/2 cup flour
2 eggs, beaten
1 cup dry bread crumbs
1/2 cup dry white wine

Preheat oven to 350º F.

Place each chicken breast between two pieces of waxed paper and flatten to
about 1/8" thickness. If you have the small fillet strip, keep it separate, remove
the tendon and flatten. Sprinkle the chicken with seasoned salt.

Whip the butter until fluffy. Add the oregano, marjoram and parsley. Spread
the butter mixture on the cheese slices, using about 1/2 of the butter mixture.

Place a cheese slice on a chicken breast and cover it with the fillet strip.
Carefully roll up the chicken so the cheese doesn't leak out while baking. Coat
the rolls with flour, dip in egg and roll in bread crumbs. Place in a baking dish
and bake, uncovered for 20 minutes.

Melt the remaining butter mixture and stir in the wine. Pour it over the chicken
and continue baking approximately 15 minutes longer. Serve, spooning the
sauce over the top or on the side.

Serves 8.

NOTE: This recipe can be made a day ahead and baked just before serving.

Page sponsored by Dr. and Mrs. Joel Boriskin and Family

Prime Thyme Chicken

6 chicken breasts, halved, skinned and boned
Seasoned flour*
3 tablespoons butter
3 tablespoons olive oil
1/2 cup dry white wine
1 tablespoon lemon juice
1 cup heavy cream
1/2 teaspoon dried thyme
4 tablespoons minced fresh parsley
Salt and pepper
1 lemon, sliced
1 tablespoon capers, rinsed and drained

Preheat oven to 200° F.

Place the chicken between sheets of plastic wrap and pound to 1/4" thickness. Coat with seasoned flour. In a skillet over medium heat, brown chicken pieces in butter and oil until done. Remove to a warm platter and place in the oven.

Add the wine and lemon juice to the skillet and simmer, stirring to blend in the browned particles. Boil to reduce the liquid by half. Add the cream, thyme and 2 tablespoons of the parsley. Simmer to thicken the sauce, adding any meat juices from warming platter. Season the sauce to taste. Pour over the chicken and garnish with the remaining parsley, the lemon slices and the capers.

Serves 6.

*Season flour with salt, pepper, cayenne pepper, paprika, rosemary and/or oregano.

Page sponsored by Rose Associates, Landscape Architects, Inc., Walnut Creek 945-1112

Renaissance Chicken

4 chicken breasts, halved,
skinned and boned

Filling
1 cup chopped cooked ham
1/2 cup chopped green onion
1/4 cup fresh bread crumbs
2 tablespoons chopped fresh parsley
2 tablespoons melted butter
1/2 teaspoon salt
1/2 teaspoon tarragon
1/8 teaspoon pepper

Coating
1 cup fresh bread crumbs
1/2 teaspoon tarragon
1/4 teaspoon salt
1 teaspoon paprika
2 eggs, beaten
1/2 cup butter

Flatten the chicken breasts to 1/4" thickness. In a medium bowl, combine all of the filling ingredients. Place 2 tablespoons of the filling on each piece of chicken. Fold the sides over the filling and then roll jellyroll fashion. Set aside.

Mix the bread crumbs, tarragon, salt and paprika. Dip each chicken roll in the beaten egg and then in the bread crumb mixture, coating evenly. To set the coating, chill chicken in the freezer for 10-15 minutes.

Preheat oven to 375° F.

Melt the butter in a 9" x 13" baking dish in the oven. Add the chicken, turning to coat. Bake 50 minutes.

Serves 6 - 8.

Polenta Strata

1 onion, diced
4 tablespoons olive oil
1 red bell pepper, diced
2 cloves garlic, finely chopped
4 zucchini, finely diced
4 quarts chicken stock
4 cups polenta
Butter
1 pound chicken, cooked and shredded
2 cups grated mozzarella cheese
1/2 cup grated parmesan cheese

Preheat oven to 350º F.

Sauté the onion in olive oil until translucent. Add the bell pepper, garlic and zucchini, and continue cooking until the zucchini is tender. Set aside.
In a large pot, bring the chicken stock to a boil. Gradually stir in the polenta. Reduce the heat and simmer, stirring constantly until the stock is completely absorbed and the consistency is fairly stiff. Remove from the heat.

Generously butter a 9" x 13" baking dish. Spread 1/2 of the polenta into the bottom of the dish. Spread the sautéed vegetables over the polenta. Sprinkle the chicken and 1 cup of the mozzarella cheese over the vegetable layer. Spread remaining polenta over the top. Top with remaining mozzarella and parmesan cheese. Bake uncovered for 45 minutes. Cut into squares and serve.

Serves 8.

VARIATION: Any vegetable can be substituted for the sautéed zucchini, such as cooked spinach or chard. Spicy sausage may be substituted for the chicken or the recipe may be made with no meat.

Maple Roast Turkey
with Corn Bread Stuffing

Turkey Stock
Neck and giblets of turkey
8 cups cold water
3 celery stalks, chopped
1 onion, chopped
2 parsley sprigs

In a heavy medium saucepan, combine all the ingredients and bring to a boil, skimming the surface occasionally. Reduce the heat and simmer for approximately 3 hours. Strain the stock and reserve the giblets for the stuffing.

Parsley-Sage Corn Bread
1 cup corn meal
1 cup flour
1 tablespoon baking powder
1 tablespoon sugar
1 teaspoon salt
1 cup milk
3 tablespoons butter, melted
1 egg
1 tablespoon chopped fresh parsley
1 tablespoon thinly sliced fresh sage leaves

Preheat oven to 400° F.

Grease a 9" square baking pan. In a large bowl, combine the first five ingredients. In another bowl, combine all remaining ingredients. Add them to the dry ingredients and mix until just combined. Pour into the prepared pan. Bake until a tester inserted in the center comes out clean, approximately 20 minutes. Serve bread warm or to use it in the stuffing, crumble it into coarse crumbs and dry **overnight** on a baking sheet.

Page sponsored by Diablo Foods of Quality, Lafayette 283-0737

Corn Bread Stuffing

5 tablespoons unsalted butter

1 large onion, chopped

3 stalks celery, chopped

3/4 cup coarsely chopped, vacuum packed, roasted chestnuts

1/2 teaspoon dried thyme, crumbled

1/4 teaspoon dried sage, crumbled

3 tablespoons chopped fresh parsley

1 tablespoon thinly sliced fresh sage leaves

4 cups coarse corn bread crumbs (recipe included)

3/4 cup chopped turkey giblets, reserved from the stock

1 extra large egg

Salt and pepper

1/2 - 3/4 cup turkey stock (recipe included)

In a large, heavy skillet, melt the butter over medium heat. Add the onion, celery, chestnuts, thyme and dried sage. Stirring occasionally, cook until the onion is translucent. Add the parsley, fresh sage leaves and stir an additional 2 minutes. Transfer to a large bowl and mix in corn bread crumbs. Add giblets and egg. Season with salt and pepper. Add enough of the stock to moisten slightly. Cool completely.

Maple Butter Glaze

1/2 cup unsalted butter

3 tablespoons minced fresh ginger

1/2 cup pure maple syrup

1/2 cup warm water

1 tablespoon snipped fresh chives

In a heavy saucepan, melt the butter over low heat. Stirring occasionally, add the ginger and cook until tender, approximately 5 minutes. Add syrup, water and simmer for 10 minutes. Stir in chives. Cool completely.

Turkey

1 16-18 pound turkey, neck
  and giblets reserved for stock
Salt
1 tablespoon minced fresh rosemary

Freshly ground pepper
Fresh mint leaves
Fresh sage leaves
Fresh herb sprigs
Fresh cranberries

Preheat oven to 325º F.

Position one rack in the center of the oven and one rack in the lower third of the oven. Rub the turkey inside and out with salt, rosemary and pepper. Fill the cavity with stuffing. Gently separate the breast skin from the meat by running hands under the skin. Dip the mint and sage leaves in the maple butter glaze and slide them under the turkey skin in a decorative pattern. Truss the turkey.

Brush generously with some of the glaze. Slide the turkey into a large, heavy, unglazed brown paper bag. Tie the bag closed.

Place the turkey in a roasting pan and place the pan on the center oven rack. Place another baking pan containing 1 1/2" of water on the lower rack. Cook the turkey for about 5 hours.

Slit the top of the bag open, exposing the turkey. Baste with the remaining glaze and cook until a meat thermometer inserted into a thigh registers 170º F., approximately 30 minutes. Transfer the turkey to a heated platter and let it stand for 30 minutes. For the sauce, strain and degrease the turkey drippings. Garnish turkey with herb sprigs and berries. Serve, passing the sauce separately.

Serves 12.

NOTE: This makes a great dinner for Thanksgiving. The flavors are wonderful and the maple syrup glaze contributes a beautiful mahogany color. Since this is a very time consuming recipe it is recommended that the stock and corn bread be made the night before.

Curried Turkey Croissant
with Cranberry Chutney

Turkey Filling

2 cups cooked turkey breast, cubed

1/2 cup chopped celery

1/4 cup raisins

1/4 cup shredded coconut

1/4 cup peanuts

1 tablespoon curry powder

2 tablespoons chopped green onions

2 tablespoons chopped parsley

1/2 cup mayonnaise

1/2 cup sour cream

Salt and pepper

6 fresh croissants

Cranberry Chutney

1/2 cup cider vinegar

2 1/4 cups light brown sugar

3/4 teaspoon curry powder

1/2 teaspoon ground ginger

1/4 teaspoon ground cloves

1/4 teaspoon ground allspice

1/2 teaspoon cinnamon

2 lemons, rind and pith discarded, sliced

2 oranges, rind and pith discarded, sliced

1 large apple, peeled and chopped

6 cups fresh cranberries

1/2 cup raisins

1/2 cup dried apricots, chopped

1/2 cup chopped walnuts

Mix all the turkey filling ingredients and chill for 1 hour. Slice the croissants in half and fill with turkey mixture.

To prepare the chutney, heat the vinegar and sugar in a 3 quart saucepan until dissolved. Add the remaining ingredients. Simmer uncovered on low heat for 20-30 minutes, until the cranberries pop and the apples are tender. Chill and keep refrigerated until ready to use. Serve as an accompaniment to the turkey croissants.

Serves 6.

Page sponsored by Mills College Conference Center and Chapel, Oakland
Karen Maggio and Tommiette Rey

Brown Rice Jambalaya

2 1/2 pounds boneless, skinless
chicken thighs

1/2 pound diced ham or bacon

1 pound Cajun sausage or chorizo

3 garlic cloves, minced

1 onion, peeled and chopped

1 green bell pepper, chopped

1 1/2 cups raw brown rice

1/2 teaspoon dried oregano

1/2 teaspoon dried thyme

1/2 teaspoon filé powder

1/2 teaspoon ground black pepper

1/4 teaspoon cayenne pepper

1/4 teaspoon ground cumin

2 tomatoes, peeled and puréed

3 cups chicken broth

Salt and pepper

1/2 pound raw shrimp, peeled, deveined

Cut the chicken into bite-size pieces. In a 4 quart stockpot, cook the bacon until crispy. Over medium heat, add the chicken to the bacon and cook until the chicken turns pale, approximately 4 minutes. Remove the bacon and chicken with a slotted spoon and place on paper toweling. Set aside. Add sausage to the stock pot and brown for approximately 6-8 minutes. Remove sausage to paper toweling. Drain and discard the drippings, reserving 2 tablespoons in the stock pot.

Add the garlic, onion and green pepper to the stock pot and stir over low heat until softened, approximately 10 minutes. Add the rice and cook over low heat for 2 minutes. Stir in herbs, spices, tomatoes and broth and heat to boiling. Reduce the heat to low. Cover and cook 15-20 minutes.

Cut the sausage into 1/4" thick round slices. Add the sausage, bacon and chicken to the rice. Cover and cook until rice is tender, approximately 20 minutes. Liquid may not be totally absorbed. Season to taste. Add shrimp. Cover pot and cook an additional 8-10 minutes. Remove from heat and let stand 5 minutes.

Serves 6.

Page sponsored by The Mohan Family

Cioppino

1/4 cup olive oil

1 bunch green onions, chopped

4 yellow onions, chopped

1/4 cup chopped fresh parsley

1 cup minced celery hearts or tops

1 red or green bell pepper, chopped

4 large garlic cloves, minced

4 large tomatoes, peeled and chopped

1 cup red wine (Merlot preferred)

1 tablespoon red wine vinegar

15 ounces tomato sauce

3 ounces tomato paste

1 cup clam juice

1/4 teaspoon allspice

1/2 teaspoon cinnamon

1/4 teaspoon oregano

1/2 teaspoon rosemary

1/2 teaspoon thyme

1 small bay leaf

Salt and freshly ground pepper

1/4 cup white wine

6 clams, well scrubbed

6 mussels, well scrubbed

1/2 pound firm white fish, cubed

6 large prawns

1 small crab, cooked, cleaned, cracked and disjointed

In a skillet, sauté the first six ingredients in olive oil until tender, approximately 5 minutes. Add the tomatoes and simmer for an additional 10 minutes. Place the sautéed mixture in a large stock pot and add red wine, vinegar, tomato sauce, tomato paste, clam juice and all of the spices. Simmer for 1/2 hour. Add the white wine and bring to a boil. A small amount of water may be added at this point if the sauce is too thick. Add the clams, mussels, white fish and cook for 3 minutes. Add the prawns and crab and cook for an additional 3 minutes. Remove from the heat and serve.

Serves 4-6.

Page sponsored by Cal & Sue Adams of Adams & Co.
General Contractors & Real Estate Brokers, Lafayette 283-7866

Kona Coast Mahi Mahi

1 1/2 pounds mahi mahi
Salt and pepper
1/4 cup flour
3/4 cup macadamia nuts,
   finely chopped
1 egg
1 tablespoon water
2 tablespoons butter
2 tablespoons olive oil
Lime slices

Season the fish with salt and pepper. Lightly coat the fish with flour. Pour the nuts into a shallow dish. In a bowl, beat together the egg and water. Dip the fish in the egg mixture, then roll in the nuts until evenly coated on both sides.

In a large skillet, over medium high heat, melt the butter and oil. Add the fillets and pan fry 3-4 minutes on each side until the outside is browned and the fish tests done. Garnish with lime slices.

Serves 4-6.

Fresh Catch

1/4 cup butter

2 tablespoons lemon juice

1 tablespoon minced chives

1/2 teaspoon tarragon

1/2 teaspoon dry mustard

1/2 teaspoon pepper

1/8 teaspoon garlic powder

1 pound fish fillets

In a frying pan, melt the butter over medium heat. Stir in the lemon juice and seasonings. Sauté the fish for about 8 minutes, or until it flakes with a fork.

Serves 4.

Page sponsored by Sierra Boat Co., Carnelian Bay
In honor of Katie & Kristina Sutherland

Connecticut Scallops and Shrimp

2 tablespoons butter
1/2 pound mushrooms, sliced
2 pounds fresh bay scallops
1 cup seasoned dry bread crumbs
1/2 pound cooked bay shrimp
3 cups heavy cream
Paprika
Chopped fresh parsley
Lemon slices

Preheat oven to 350° F.

In a frying pan, melt the butter and sauté the mushrooms until soft. Set aside.

Coat the scallops with 1/2 of the bread crumbs. In a buttered casserole dish, arrange the scallops in a single layer. Cover the scallops with the shrimp and mushrooms. Pour the cream over the scallops to cover evenly. Sprinkle with paprika. Bake for approximately 45 minutes, until brown and bubbly.

Garnish with chopped parsley and lemon slices.

Serves 8.

Scampi

3/4 pound medium size raw shrimp,
   shelled and deveined
6 tablespoons butter
1 tablespoon olive oil
1 tablespoon minced green onion
5 cloves garlic, minced
2 teaspoons fresh lemon juice
1/4 teaspoon salt
2 tablespoons fresh minced parsley
1/4 teaspoon grated lemon peel
Dash of Tabasco sauce
Salt and pepper
Lemon wedges

Rinse the shrimp and pat them dry. Set aside.

In a large frying pan, melt the butter and oil over medium heat. Stir in the onion, garlic, lemon juice and salt. Cook over low heat until bubbly. Add the shrimp and cook, stirring occasionally, until they turn pink. Blend in the parsley, lemon peel and Tabasco. Season with salt and pepper. Serve over steamed rice, and garnish with lemon wedges.

Serves 2.

Page sponsored by The Grodin Family - Marshall, Anne, Mathew and Lori

Mussels in White Wine

4 pounds mussels, rinsed,
 scrubbed & beards removed
4-5 cloves garlic, chopped
3 shallots, chopped
1/2 cup chopped fresh parsley
1/2 cup butter
1/4 cup dry white wine
Freshly ground pepper
1 cup heavy cream

In a large frying pan, place all ingredients except the cream. Cover and cook over high heat, shaking the pan 2-3 times to blend the ingredients. Cook until the mussels open, approximately 5 minutes.

Discard any unopened mussels. Remove opened mussels to individual soup plates, reserving the liquid in the pan. Add the cream to the pan and heat through. Ladle the sauce over the mussels and serve.

Serves 4.

VARIATION: This is excellent served over pasta if the sauce is thickened by increasing the cooking time after the addition of the cream.

Page sponsored by the Happy Valley Improvement Association, Lafayette

Marinades

Summer Basil Marinade

1/3 cup lemon juice

2 tablespoons Dijon mustard

1/2 cup finely chopped fresh basil

1/3 cup chopped chives

2 tablespoons dry white wine

1/2 tablespoon salt

1/4 teaspoon freshly ground pepper

1 cup olive oil

2 cloves garlic, crushed

In a bowl, combine all ingredients except the oil. Whisk in the oil gradually until blended. Marinate fish or chicken for 3 hours. Grill or broil as desired.

Florida Citrus Marinade

1 teaspoon red pepper flakes, crushed

2 teaspoons fresh dill, chopped

1/4 cup minced onion

3 cloves garlic, minced

Salt and pepper

Juice and zest of 1 orange

Juice and zest of 1 lemon

Juice and zest of 1 lime

1/3 cup olive oil

3 tablespoons chopped parsley

In a bowl, mash together the first 5 ingredients. Stir in all the citrus to blend. Whisk in the olive oil and add the parsley.

Marinate fish or chicken for 1-2 hours. Grill or broil as desired.

Page sponsored by Allan R. Horeis Structural Engineers, Inc., Walnut Creek 935-8001

Fish Sauce Medley

Ginger-Lime Sauce

1/2 cup dry white wine
1/2 cup chicken broth
2 tablespoons minced shallots
1 teaspoon grated fresh ginger
1 teaspoon grated lime peel
1/2 cup heavy cream
1/4 cup unsalted butter
Grilled Fish
Lime slices

In a skillet, combine the wine, broth, shallots, ginger and lime peel. Bring to a boil and cook, uncovered, to reduce by one half. Add the cream and boil, uncovered, until reduced to 3/4 cup. Lower the heat to medium and add the butter, stirring constantly, until blended. Spoon onto individual plates, top with grilled fish and garnish with lime slices.

Black and Red Salsa

3 tomatoes, peeled and diced
1/2 cup diced black olives
1/3 cup sliced green onions
1 garlic clove, minced
6 tablespoons olive oil
2 tablespoons rice vinegar
Grilled Fish
Fresh cilantro sprigs

Cook first six ingredients in a double boiler over simmering water. Heat through, stirring occasionally. Spoon over grilled fish and garnish with cilantro.

Page sponsored by William L. Strauss, M.D., Moraga 376-5161

Avocado Butter

1/2 cup butter, softened
1 ripe avocado, mashed
5 tablespoons fresh lime juice
2 tablespoons minced fresh parsley
2 garlic cloves, minced
Salt and white pepper
Grilled Fish
Lemon wedges

In a small bowl, beat the butter until soft and fluffy. Blend in the avocado, lime juice, parsley and garlic. Season to taste. Cover and refrigerate until ready to serve. Top each piece of grilled fish with a dollop of avocado butter. Garnish with lemon wedges.

Page sponsored by a Friend of the Cookbook

Pacific Coast Pasta

1/2 cup plus 1 tablespoon unsalted butter
6 oil packed sundried tomatoes, cut in thirds
1/4 pound mushrooms, thinly sliced
1 clove garlic, minced
3/4 cup heavy cream
3/4 cup freshly grated parmesan cheese
1/4 teaspoon nutmeg
Freshly ground pepper
1/2 pound cooked bay shrimp
1/4 cup pine nuts
1 pound fresh herb fettucine, cooked al dente

In a medium sauté pan over low heat, melt 1 tablespoon of butter and sauté the tomatoes, mushrooms and garlic. Set aside.

In a saucepan, slowly melt 1/2 cup butter . Stir in the cream and heat just to boiling. Add 1/2 cup of the cheese, the nutmeg, pepper and shrimp.

Toss together the pasta, sauce, shrimp mixture and pine nuts. Sprinkle with the remaining parmesan cheese.

Serves 4-6.

Page sponsored by the Lafayette School District Administrative Council

Linguine with Clam Sauce

1/2 cup butter

1/4 cup olive oil

6 cloves garlic, minced

1 onion, chopped

1/4 pound mushrooms, thinly sliced

24 ounces canned chopped clams

1/4 cup dry white wine

1/4 cup chopped fresh basil

1/2 cup chopped fresh parsley

1/4 teaspoon crushed red pepper flakes

1/4 teaspoon white pepper

1/4 teaspoon lemon pepper

6 ounces marinated artichoke hearts,
     drained and chopped

4 ounces sliced ripe olives

1 tablespoon capers

1 pound fresh linguine, cooked al dente

Freshly grated parmesan cheese

12-18 steamed fresh clams

In a 2 quart saucepan, melt the butter and add the oil. Quickly sauté the garlic,
onion and mushrooms. Drain the juice from the clams into the butter mixture.
Add the wine, basil, parsley, pepper seasonings, artichoke hearts, olives and capers.
Simmer for 5 minutes. Add the clams and heat through.

Toss the sauce with the pasta. Sprinkle with parmesan cheese and garnish with
steamed clams.

Serves 6.

Page sponsored by Safeway, Inc., Fremont

Pasta Puttanesca
From Tourelle, Lafayette

6 ounces extra virgin olive oil
3 cloves garlic, minced
3 anchovy fillets, minced
4 Roma tomatoes, diced
2 tablespoons capers
16 Kalamata olives, pitted, and finely chopped
Salt and pepper
Fresh pasta, cooked al dente
6 fresh basil leaves, chopped
Pinch of red pepper flakes

In a large sauté pan, heat the olive oil. Add the garlic and anchovies. Sauté on medium heat for 2 minutes. Add the tomatoes, capers, and olives. Reduce the heat and simmer 10 minutes. Season the sauce with salt and pepper. Add the sauce to the pasta and toss with the basil and red pepper flakes.
Serve immediately.

Page sponsored by Bedford Properties, Lafayette
Peter B. Bedford

Penne with Swiss Chard

1 pound penne or other small pasta
1 pound Swiss chard, washed and cut
   into 1" strips, stems included
6 cloves garlic, minced
1/4 teaspoon crushed red pepper flakes
1/3 cup olive oil
2 teaspoons salt
Seasoned bread crumbs

In a large pot of boiling salted water, cook the Swiss chard and pasta al dente.
Drain.

While the pasta is cooking, sauté the garlic and red pepper flakes in the olive oil
until the garlic is lightly browned. Stir in the salt and keep warm.

Place the pasta and chard in a large bowl. Add the seasoned oil and mix well.
Sprinkle with the bread crumbs and serve.

Serves 8.

VARIATION: This is also delicious when sautéed slices of a spicy sausage such
as andouille are added.

Lasagne with Tomato Herb Sauce
From Mudd's Restaurant, San Ramon

Tomato Herb Sauce

1 cup chopped celery

1 onion, finely chopped

1 cup chopped carrots

1 tablespoon minced garlic

1/4 cup olive oil

4 cups canned tomatoes

4 cups diced tomatoes

1 tablespoon sugar

1 cup red wine

White pepper

Thyme

Oregano

1/2 bunch fresh basil, chopped

Bay leaf

1/2 bunch fresh parsley, chopped

Red pepper flakes

Lasagne

3 tablespoons olive oil

1 cup thinly sliced zucchini

1/4 cup chopped red bell pepper

1/4 cup thinly sliced red cabbage

1/2 cup chopped red onion

1 tablespoon chopped garlic

1 egg

Pinch of nutmeg

Pinch of chopped garden herbs

1 cup ricotta low fat cheese

1/8 cup grated parmesan

1/8 cup grated low fat mozzarella

Salt and pepper

Tomato Herb Sauce (recipe included)

Pasta sheets or lasagne noodles,
  cooked al dente

Grated mozzarella cheese for topping

Grated parmesan cheese for topping

Sauce: Sauté vegetables and garlic slowly in olive oil for 10 minutes. Add the remaining ingredients and simmer for 2 hours.

Lasagne: In the olive oil, sauté the vegetables and herbs together until just barely done. Season to taste. Cool. Beat the egg and add the cheeses. Combine with the cooled vegetables. Layer pasta with vegetable-cheese mixture and tomato herb sauce. Repeat as necessary. Top with mozzarella and parmesan cheeses. Bake at 350º F. for 35-40 minutes.

NOTE: Fresh skinned and seeded vine ripe tomatoes may be used during the season. This sauce is very good on chicken and fish.

Page sponsored by Mudd's Restaurant, San Ramon   837-9387
In honor of the wonderful children of Lafayette

Elisabeth's Chili Relleno Casserole

From Kaffee Barbara, Lafayette

21 ounces canned whole green chilies,
   split open
4 cups shredded cheddar cheese
4 cups shredded Monterey Jack cheese
4 eggs
1 1/2 - 2 tablespoons flour
12 ounces evaporated milk
1/2 teaspoon salt
1/2 teaspoon pepper
Avocado wedges
Sour cream
Salsa

Preheat oven to 350º F.

Lightly grease a 9" x 13" casserole and line it with split green chilies. Layer the cheeses. Mix the eggs, flour, evaporated milk, salt and pepper. Pour the egg mixture over the cheese.

Place the casserole in a larger pan. Place both in the oven and fill the larger pan half full with water.

Bake for 35-45 minutes. Casserole should be slightly puffed in the center. Serve with avocado, sour cream and salsa.

Vegetarian Burritos with Peanut Sauce

Peanut Sauce

6 tablespoons peanut butter

10 tablespoons vegetable oil

8 tablespoons soy sauce

8 tablespoons sugar

8 teaspoons white vinegar

2 teaspoons Oriental sesame oil

1 teaspoon cayenne pepper

4 tablespoons minced green onion

4 tablespoons minced fresh cilantro

Burritos

1 tablespoon vegetable oil

2 medium zucchini, sliced

1/2 cup diced green bell pepper

1/2 cup diced red bell pepper

1/4 pound mushrooms, sliced

1 carrot, shredded

2 green onions, sliced

10 ounces frozen corn, thawed

3 cups cooked brown rice

Peanut sauce (recipe included)

12 flour tortillas

Mix the peanut butter and oil in a food processor. Add the remaining sauce ingredients and process until blended.

In a large frying pan, heat the oil and sauté the zucchini, peppers, mushrooms, carrot, and onion until slightly limp. Add the corn and brown rice and heat through. Mix in 1/4 cup of the peanut sauce and heat through. To serve, spread a small amount of peanut sauce on a tortilla, add some of the vegetable and rice mixture and roll up burrito style.

Serves 6.

VEGETABLES
& SIDE DISHES

Green Beans with Garlic
Mint Marinated Grilled Red Onions
Deviled Tomatoes
Gingered Butternut Squash
Fourth of July Baked Squash
Sherried Sweets
Orange Praline Yams
Winter Garden Vegetables
Croûte de Champignons
Peperonata
Ratatouille
Port Glazed Carrots
Spinach Bake
Gratin Dauphinois
Hacienda Potatoes
Potato Pancakes
Layered Rice Monterey
Wild Rice and Mushroom Casserole
Herbed Lentils and Rice
Curried Couscous
Portugese Beans
Bonanza Baked Beans

Green Beans with Garlic

4 teaspoons soy sauce

1 teaspoon sugar

1 tablespoon dry sherry or water

1 tablespoon sesame seeds

1 1/2 tablespoons vegetable oil

3 cloves garlic minced

1 tablespoon fresh minced ginger

1 pound green beans, ends trimmed,
　　cut diagonally into 2" lengths

In a small bowl, combine the soy sauce, sugar and sherry. Set aside.

Using a wok or frying pan over low heat, cook the sesame seeds, stirring constantly until lightly browned, approximately 3 minutes. Remove from the pan and set aside.

Increase the heat to medium high and add oil to the wok. When the oil is hot, stir in the garlic, ginger and beans. Cook, stirring for approximately 90 seconds. Add the soy mixture. Cover the pan and reduce the heat to medium. Cook, stirring occasionally, until the beans are tender but crisp, approximately 7 minutes. Uncover, increase the heat to high and boil, stirring, until liquid has almost evaporated, approximately 1-3 minutes.

Pour the beans onto a platter and sprinkle with the toasted sesame seeds.

VARIATION: For a spicy version, add red pepper flakes.

Mint Marinated Grilled Red Onions

3 red onions
2 teaspoons dried mint, crumbled
2 teaspoons dried oregano, crumbled
1/2 teaspoon salt
1 teaspoon sugar
1/4 cup white wine vinegar
2 tablespoons olive oil

Slice the onions into 1/2" thick slices, being careful not to let them separate into individual rings. In a shallow casserole large enough to hold the onions in one layer, whisk together all remaining ingredients. Add the onions, cover and marinate, turning occasionally for at least 3 hours or **overnight.**

Remove the onions from the marinade and grill on a well-oiled rack over glowing coals. Using a metal spatula, turn them occasionally to prevent burning. Cook for 8 minutes or until tender. Transfer to a heated platter. Serve with grilled meats, poultry or fish.

Page sponsored by Douglas E. Cowden, D.D.S., Lafayette 283-0313

Deviled Tomatoes

4 tablespoons butter
1 teaspoon dry mustard
1 hard cooked egg yolk,
   riced or mashed
1 egg, slightly beaten
2 tablespoons vinegar
1/4 teaspoon salt
Dash of cayenne pepper
3 large firm tomatoes
Salt and pepper
1/2 tablespoon butter

In a double boiler bowl, cream the butter. Add the mustard, egg yolk, egg, vinegar and seasonings. Mix well. Place over simmering water, stirring constantly until thickened.

Core the tomatoes and cut into thick wedges. Sprinkle with salt and pepper. In a medium sauté pan, melt the butter and sauté the tomatoes briefly until tender.

Place the tomatoes on a serving dish and top with the sauce.

Serves 4-6.

NOTE: These are great with grilled fish.

Gingered Butternut Squash

4 large butternut squash
3 teaspoons minced fresh ginger
3 tablespoons butter
Salt and pepper

Cut the squash in half lengthwise, removing the seeds and strings. Using a melon baller, scoop balls from the squash or cut into chunks, discarding the rind. Simmer the squash for 5 minutes in boiling, salted water. Drain. Toss with butter, ginger, salt and pepper.

Serves 8-10.

NOTE: This is a good accompaniment to Roast Pork with Sausage Stuffing on page 55.

———————————— ❧ ————————————

Page sponsored by Steve & Judith Brooks
Brooks Typography, Lafayette

Fourth of July Baked Squash

3 pounds yellow summer squash,
    washed and cut into cubes
1/4 cup unsalted butter
1/2 cup chopped onion
2 eggs
1 tablespoon sugar
1 teaspoon salt
1/2 teaspoon black pepper
1/4 cup unsalted butter, melted
1/2 cup cracker meal or bread crumbs

Preheat oven to 375º F.

Boil the squash until tender and drain well. Mash the squash, adding the butter, onion, eggs, sugar, salt and pepper. Pour the mixture into a baking dish. Combine melted butter with cracker meal or bread crumbs. Sprinkle this mixture over the squash. Bake for approximately 1 hour or until heated through and brown on top.

Serves 8-10.

Page sponsored by Claudia Casey, Pacific Union Real Estate, Lafayette 284-3700 or 284-2928
"Real Estate at its Best"

115

Sherried Sweets

8 sweet potatoes, cooked and peeled

1/2 cup butter, softened

2 tablespoons brown sugar

1/3 cup cream, warmed

2 tablespoons dry sherry

Salt

White pepper

Pinch of nutmeg

2 pinches of ginger

1 teaspoon grated orange rind

2 tablespoons Seville orange marmalade

Orange juice, to taste

Preheat oven to 350° F.

Mash or rice the sweet potatoes. Beat in the butter, brown sugar, cream and sherry. Add the remaining ingredients. Bake in a 2 1/2 to 3 quart casserole for approximately 25 minutes.

Serves 8-10.

NOTE: A beautiful way to serve this is to pipe the mixture into hollowed out orange halves, garnish with cranberries and bake at 350° F. for 15-20 minutes.

Orange Praline Yams

Casserole

4 pounds yams, cooked, peeled and sliced

2/3 cup orange juice

1 tablespoon grated orange rind

4 tablespoons brandy

2 teaspoons salt

Freshly ground pepper

1 teaspoon ground ginger

1/2 cup butter, melted

1/3 cup brown sugar

3 egg yolks

Topping

2/3 cup brown sugar

1/2 cup butter, melted

1 cup chopped pecans

1 teaspoon cinnamon

Preheat oven to 350° F.

In a mixing bowl, beat the yams until smooth. Mix in the remaining casserole ingredients, beating until light and fluffy. Pour the mixture into a buttered 7" x 11" casserole or a 12" quiche dish and smooth the top. Combine all of the topping ingredients in a small bowl. Sprinkle over the yams. At this point, the casserole may be covered and refrigerated *overnight.*

Bake uncovered for 45-50 minutes, or until golden brown and bubbly. Let stand for 10 minutes before serving.

Serves 10-12.

Page sponsored by A•Plumbing Company, Lafayette 283-1773

Winter Garden Vegetables

2 cups broccoli flowerettes
2 cups cauliflower flowerettes
2 cups carrots in 1/2" slices
1/4 cup finely chopped onion
3/4 cup mayonnaise
4 tablespoons horseradish
1/4 teaspoon salt
1/4 teaspoon pepper
1/3 cup cracker crumbs
2 tablespoons butter, melted
1/8 teaspoon paprika

Preheat oven to 350º F.

Steam the broccoli, cauliflower and carrots until tender yet crisp.

Combine the onion, mayonnaise, horseradish, salt, and pepper. Add the mixture to the vegetables, tossing until well coated. Spoon into a lightly greased 2 quart baking dish. Combine cracker crumbs, butter and paprika. Sprinkle crumb mixture over vegetables. Bake for 10-15 minutes.

Serves 6-8.

Croûte de Champignons

4 slices sweet French bread

2 tablespoons unsalted butter

1 shallot, finely chopped

1 garlic clove, crushed

1/2 pound fresh mushrooms, diced

Pinch of salt

Freshly ground pepper

2 tablespoons dry white wine

1/2 cup heavy cream

2 tablespoons Swiss cheese, shredded

1/2 tablespoon bread crumbs

1/4 teaspoon unsalted butter

Arrange the bread slices in 2 au gratin dishes and toast under the broiler until golden. In a saucepan, melt 2 tablespoons of butter and sauté the shallot and garlic until translucent. Stir in the mushrooms and season with salt and pepper. Cook over medium heat until the mushrooms are browned. Add the wine and simmer for 1 minute. Stir in the cream and simmer until the sauce is thickened.

Spoon the mushroom mixture over the toasted bread. Sprinkle with cheese and bread crumbs. Top with 1/4 teaspoon butter and broil until golden.

Serves 2.

Peperonata

2 tablespoons butter

1/4 cup olive oil

2 pounds onions, chopped

2 pounds green and red bell peppers,
   cut into strips

56 ounces canned whole tomatoes,
   drained and chopped

1 teaspoon red wine vinegar

1 teaspoon salt

1 teaspoon pepper

In a large, heavy skillet, melt the butter with the oil over moderate heat. Add the onions and sauté. Stir in the peppers. Reduce the heat, cover and cook for 20 minutes. Add the tomatoes, vinegar, salt and pepper. Cover and cook an additional 20 minutes. Remove the lid and continue to cook over moderate heat, stirring occasionally until most of the liquid has evaporated. Serve hot as a vegetable dish or cold as an appetizer.

Serves 10.

Ratatouille

3 tablespoons olive oil
1 onion, sliced
1 bell pepper, green, red or yellow, sliced
3 cloves garlic, chopped
1 eggplant, cut into strips
2 zucchini, sliced into rounds
1/2 pound green beans, cut into 2" pieces
16 ounces canned tomatoes
1/2 teaspoon marjoram
1/2 teaspoon oregano
1/2 teaspoon basil
Salt and pepper
Cayenne pepper

NOTE: Quantities do not have to be exact.

In a large pot, heat the olive oil over medium heat. Add the onions, peppers and garlic. Cook until the onions are translucent, being careful not to burn the mixture. Add the remaining ingredients. Cover and simmer to soften the vegetables.

Lower the heat and simmer uncovered, reducing to desired consistency. Stir occasionally to avoid sticking or burning.

VARIATION: Scallops, clams or shrimp may be added. This is also delicious when topped with cheese.

Port Glazed Carrots

1 pound baby carrots
4 tablespoons Tawny port
3 tablespoons balsamic vinegar
3 tablespoons honey
Salt
1/4 cup chopped fresh parsley

Steam or blanch the carrots until tender but crisp. Drain and set aside.

In a frying pan, combine port, vinegar, honey and salt and bring to a sizzle over high heat. Add the carrots. Lower the heat to medium. Shaking the pan occasionally, cook until the sauce thickens and carrots are covered with a rich bronze coating, approximately 8-10 minutes. Add parsley and stir to coat.

Serves 4-6.

Page sponsored by Eliot, Susan and Christopher Hudson

Spinach Bake

1/2 cup butter
1 quart small curd cottage cheese
4 eggs
5 tablespoons flour
1/2 pound grated cheese - Cheddar,
    Jack or mixture
1 garlic clove, minced
Salt and pepper
2 tablespoons Danish fried onions
2 - 10 ounce packages frozen chopped
    spinach, thawed and drained
2 tablespoons butter
1/2 cup bread crumbs

Preheat oven to 350º F.

Cut the butter into coarse pieces. Add the cottage cheese, eggs, flour, cheese, garlic, salt, pepper, onions and mix well. Stir in the spinach and pour into a well-greased casserole. In a frying pan, melt the remaining butter, add bread crumbs and brown. Top the spinach with the bread crumb mixture.

Bake for 1 hour.

Serves 6.

Page sponsored by Blodgett's Carpet & Linoleum, Lafayette 284-4807

Gratin Dauphinois

2 1/2 cups cream

1 tablespoon butter

3 large cloves garlic, crushed

5 large baking potatoes,
   peeled and thinly sliced

Salt

Freshly ground pepper

1 1/2 cups parmesan cheese,
   freshly grated

Preheat oven to 325º F.

In a saucepan, combine cream, butter and garlic and simmer for 15 minutes. Butter a 4 cup au gratin dish and arrange thinly sliced potatoes in the dish layering potatoes, salt, pepper and 1 cup of the parmesan cheese. Pour the creamed mixture on top and sprinkle with the remaining parmesan cheese. The casserole will be very soupy. Cover dish with foil and bake for 1 1/2 hours or until all the liquid disappears. Uncover and bake for an additional 15 minutes to brown.

Hacienda Potatoes

6 cups cooked potatoes, peeled and diced
2 green onions, chopped
1/2 pound Monterey Jack cheese, shredded
1 medium green bell pepper, diced
1 cup chopped fresh parsley
1 teaspoon salt
1/4 cup vegetable oil

Preheat oven to 350º F.

Combine all ingredients. Pour into a greased 8" x 12" baking dish and bake for 40 minutes.

Serves 10.

Page sponsored by Moraga Veterinary Hospital, Moraga 376-1121
William Kidd, D.V.M

Potato Pancakes

4 large russet potatoes
2 tablespoons flour
1/2 cup dry Italian bread crumbs
2 tablespoons chopped fresh parsley
2 tablespoons chopped onion
1/4 teaspoon paprika
1 clove garlic, chopped
1 tablespoon grated parmesan cheese
1/4 cup milk
1 egg, beaten
3 tablespoons vegetable oil

Boil whole potatoes until just tender. Chill **overnight.**

Peel the potatoes and grate them into a large bowl. Toss the grated potatoes with the flour. Add breadcrumbs, parsley, onion, paprika, garlic and cheese, and mix together with your hands. Combine the milk and egg, and add to the potato mixture.

Form the mixture into thin patties. On a large griddle, heat the oil and brown the potato patties until crispy, turning only once.

Serves 4.

Page sponsored by Papyrus, Lafayette 283-2391
Fine greeting cards and papers

Layered Rice Monterey

2 cups cooked rice

7 ounces canned chopped green chilies

3 cups shredded Monterey Jack cheese

3 medium zucchini, sliced

1 large tomato sliced

2 cups sour cream

1 teaspoon oregano

1 teaspoon salt

2 tablespoons chopped green pepper

2 tablespoons chopped green onion

1 tablespoon chopped parsley

Preheat oven to 350° F.

Place the rice in a buttered casserole. Layer it with chilies, 2 cups of the cheese, zucchini and tomato. Combine the sour cream with the oregano, salt, green pepper, onion and parsley. Pour over the zucchini and tomato layer and top with the remaining cheese.

Bake for 30 minutes.

Serves 8.

———————— ❧ ————————

Page sponsored by Alida M. Robinson in memory of her loving Mother

Wild Rice and Mushroom Casserole

1/4 cup butter
1/2 cup wild rice, rinsed and drained
1/4 cup brown rice
1/3 cup chopped onion
1/2 pound mushrooms, sliced
1/3 cup pine nuts
2 cups chicken broth

Preheat oven to 325° F.

In a large ovenproof skillet, melt the butter. Sauté the rices, onion, mushrooms, and pine nuts over medium heat until the onion and mushrooms are soft. Pour the broth over the rice mixture and cover tightly. Bake 1 1/2 hours or until rice is tender.

Serves 8.

Page sponsored by Westinghouse Electric Corporation, Lafayette
In memory of George Westinghouse

Herbed Lentils and Rice

3/4 cup dry lentils
1/2 cup brown rice
2 2/3 cups chicken broth
1/4 cup dry white wine
3/4 cup chopped onion
1/2 teaspoon dried basil, crushed
1/4 teaspoon oregano
1/8 teaspoon pepper
1/2 cup shredded Swiss cheese
8 strips Swiss cheese
Tomatoes, sliced
Fresh parsley

Preheat oven to 350º F.

Combine all ingredients except the strips of Swiss cheese, tomatoes and parsley. Place the mixture in an ungreased 1 1/2 quart covered casserole.

Bake covered 1 1/2 - 2 hours. Uncover and place cheese strips on top and bake until cheese melts.

Garnish with sliced tomatoes and sprigs of parsley.

Serves 4.

Page sponsored by Charles M. Salter Associates, Inc., San Francisco

Curried Couscous

1 1/2 cup chicken broth
1/2 cup golden raisins
1/4 cup lemon juice
2 tablespoons minced crystallized ginger
2 tablespoons butter
1/2 teaspoon curry powder
1 cup couscous
1/3 cup chopped celery
1/3 cup chopped green onion
2 tablespoons chopped fresh cilantro
1/3 cup chopped roasted, salted pistachio nuts
Cilantro sprigs

In a saucepan, bring the chicken broth to a boil and add the raisins, lemon juice, ginger, butter, curry powder and couscous. Cover the pan and remove from the heat. Let stand for at least 5 minutes or up to 3 hours. At this point the couscous mixture may be refrigerated until the next day.

When the couscous mixture is at room temperature, mix in celery, green onion, and chopped cilantro. Mound couscous on a platter, sprinkle with pistachios and garnish with cilantro sprigs.

Serve at room temperature.

Portuguese Beans

1 pound dried pinto beans, rinsed
6 strips bacon, diced
2 large onions, diced
8 ounces tomato sauce
1/4 cup ketchup
1/4 cup sugar
1/4 cup red wine
4 tablespoons vinegar
6 drops Tabasco sauce
1 teaspoon Italian seasoning
1/2 teaspoon cumin
2 cloves garlic, minced
1 teaspoon cinnamon
Salt and pepper

Place the beans in a large saucepan. Add the bacon and onion. Cover with water, up to 2" from the rim of the pan. Bring to a boil, reduce heat and simmer uncovered for 2-3 hours, stirring occasionally. Add more water only if the beans become too dry, as some liquid will be absorbed.

Add the remaining ingredients and continue to simmer an additional 1 to 1 1/2 hours, stirring frequently.

Serves 8-10.

NOTE: Beans are even better the next day after flavors have blended.

Bonanza Baked Beans

1/2 pound bacon, diced

2 onions, diced

3/4 cup brown sugar

1/2 cup ketchup

1/4 cup vinegar

1/4 teaspoon garlic salt

1/4 teaspoon dry mustard

1 can pork and beans

1 can butter beans and ham

1 can green lima beans, drained

1 can kidney beans, drained

1 can jalapeño navy beans (optional)

Preheat oven to 350° F.

Brown the bacon, drain well, reserving 3 tablespoons of drippings, and set aside. To the reserved bacon drippings, add the next 6 ingredients. Simmer 20 minutes. Add the remaining ingredients and the diced bacon. Pour into a casserole and bake covered for 1 hour.

Serves 10-12.

BREADS & BREAKFASTS

Raspberry Muffins
Morning Glory Muffins
Fresh Lemon Bread
Cranberry Nut Bread
Autumn Pumpkin Bread
Dad's Banana Bread
Palouse Raisin Bread
Apple Walnut Ring
Sour Cream Coffee Cake
Irish Scones
Angel Biscuits
Naan - Indian Yogurt Bread
Herbed Cheese Bread
Mexican Spoon Bread
Onion Cheese Puffs
Spinach Feta Crustless Quiche
Breakfast Cheese Strata
Eggs San Juan
Crab Omelet
Trou Pain Perdu
French Toast Soufflé
Dutch Apple Pancake
Granola

Raspberry Muffins

3 cups unbleached flour

1 1/2 tablespoons baking powder

1/2 teaspoon baking soda

1/4 teaspoon salt

4 1/2 teaspoons ground cinnamon

1 1/4 cups milk

2 eggs, well beaten

3/4 cup butter

2-3 cups raspberries

1 1/2 cups sugar

Preheat oven to 375° F.

Insert paper muffin liners into muffin tins. For jumbo-topped muffins, also grease the top flat surface of the muffin tin.

Combine the flour, baking powder, baking soda, salt and cinnamon. Make a well in the center of the mixture. Add the milk, eggs and butter to the well and stir until just combined. Fold in the berries and sugar.

Spoon the batter into the liners. For regular muffins, fill half full and for jumbo-topped muffins fill completely. Bake until the muffins test done and the tops are golden brown, approximately 20 minutes.

Makes 12-18 muffins.

NOTE: Raspberries will maintain their shape if frozen individually on a cookie sheet before preparing the recipe.

Page sponsored by Linda Murray in memory of Mom

Morning Glory Muffins

2 cups flour

1 cup sugar

2 teaspoons baking soda

1/2 teaspoon salt

2 teaspoons cinnamon

1/4 teaspoon ground cloves

1/4 teaspoon nutmeg

1/2 cup raisins

2 cups grated carrots

1 large tart green apple, peeled, cored and grated

1/2 cup slivered almonds

3 eggs

2/3 cup vegetable oil

2 teaspoons vanilla

Preheat oven to 350º F.

Insert paper muffin liners in muffin tin. For jumbo-topped muffins, also grease the top flat surface of the muffin tin.

In a bowl, mix the flour, sugar, baking soda, salt, cinnamon, cloves and nutmeg. Stir in the raisins, carrots, apple and nuts. In a separate bowl, beat the eggs, oil and vanilla to blend. Stir into the flour mixture until just combined. Divide the batter among the muffin cups, filling each 1/2 full for regular size muffins and completely full for jumbo-topped muffins.

Bake 20-22 minutes until golden brown. Cool 5 minutes. Serve at room temperature.

Fresh Lemon Bread

1/3 cup butter, softened
1/2 cup sugar
2 eggs
1 1/2 cups flour
1 teaspoon baking powder
1/2 cup milk
Rind of 1 lemon, grated
1/2 cup chopped walnuts
Juice of 1 lemon
1/3 cup sugar

Preheat oven to 350º F.

Cream the butter and sugar until fluffy. Add the eggs and blend well. Sift the flour and baking powder together. To the creamed mixture, alternately add half of the dry ingredients and half of the milk. Blend well after each addition. Repeat until totally combined. Stir in the lemon rind and nuts.

Bake in a greased 9" x 5" loaf pan for 50-60 minutes or until done. Let cool for 10 minutes. Combine the lemon juice and sugar and pour over the bread.

Serves 6 to 8.

Cranberry Nut Bread

2 cups flour
1/2 teaspoon salt
1 1/2 teaspoons baking powder
1/2 teaspoon baking soda
1 cup sugar
Juice of 1 orange
2 tablespoons melted butter
Boiling water
1 egg, beaten
Rind of 1 orange, grated
1 cup chopped walnuts
1 cup chopped fresh cranberries

Preheat oven to 325° F.

Sift the first 5 ingredients together. Set aside. Place the orange juice and butter in a 1 cup measure. Add boiling water to equal 1 cup. Pour into a large bowl, add the egg and mix thoroughly. Add the dry ingredients, mixing until just blended. Fold in the orange rind, walnuts and cranberries.

Bake in a greased 9" x 5" loaf pan for 60-75 minutes or until done.

NOTE: This bread is best if stored 1-2 days before eating.

Autumn Pumpkin Bread

3 1/2 cups flour

2 teaspoons baking soda

1 teaspoon cinnamon

1 teaspoon nutmeg

1 1/2 teaspoons salt

3 cups sugar

4 eggs, beaten

3 teaspoons vanilla

1 cup vegetable oil

2/3 cup water

2 cups canned pumpkin

1 1/2 cups golden raisins

2 cups chopped walnuts

Preheat oven to 350º F.

Sift the first 6 ingredients and make a well in the center. Add all remaining ingredients, except the raisins and walnuts. Stir together until smooth. Fold in the raisins and walnuts. Pour the batter into 3 greased and floured bread loaf pans. Bake for 1 hour.

NOTE: This recipe also makes excellent muffins.

Page sponsored by Roger and Kit Wiggins

Dad's Banana Bread

1 cup sugar
1/2 cup shortening
2 eggs
3 tablespoons cream
3 ripe bananas, mashed
1/2 teaspoon salt
1 teaspoon baking soda
2 cups flour
1 teaspoon baking powder
1/2 cup chopped nuts

Preheat oven to 350º F.

Cream the sugar and shortening until smooth. Add the eggs, cream, bananas and beat well. Sift dry ingredients and gradually stir into the banana mixture until just moistened. Fold in the nuts.

Bake in a greased and floured 9" x 5" loaf pan for 1 hour.

Page sponsored by Susan Rothenberg, TRI Realtors, Orinda 254-7777
In honor of the Lafayette School District students

Palouse Raisin Bread

1/4 cup butter, softened

1/4 cup sugar

2 eggs

1 cup small curd cottage cheese

1/2 cup raisins

2 cups flour

4 teaspoons baking powder

1/4 teaspoon baking soda

1/4 teaspoon salt

1/2 cup milk

1 teaspoon caraway seeds

Preheat oven to 375º F.

Cream the butter and sugar until fluffy. Beat in the eggs, cottage cheese and raisins. Sift together the flour, baking powder, baking soda and salt. To the creamed mixture, alternately add half of the dry ingredients and half of the milk. Blend well after each addition. Repeat until totally combined. Add the caraway seeds. Turn into a greased and floured 8" layer pan.

Bake for 10 minutes. Reduce oven heat to 350º F. and bake for an additional 40 minutes or until a toothpick inserted in the center comes out clean. Cool in the pan for 10 minutes and then invert on a rack to finish cooling.

Buckley, Patchen, Riemann & Phillips, An Accountancy Corporation
Gerald E. Patchen, Lafayette 284-5262

Apple Walnut Ring

Makes 2 Rings

Dough
1/4 cup warm water (105°-110° F.)
1 tablespoon sugar
2 packages rapid rise yeast
1/3 cup milk
1 cup butter
1/2 cup sugar
1 teaspoon salt
1 cup sour cream
4 egg yolks
5 1/2 - 6 cups flour

Filling
4 large tart green apples
2 teaspoons grated lemon zest
3 tablespoons fresh lemon juice
3/4 cup sugar
2 egg yolks, beaten
2 tablespoons flour
1/4 teaspoon cinnamon
2 tablespoons butter
1 teaspoon vanilla
1 cup chopped walnuts

Glaze
4 tablespoons cream cheese, softened
2 cups powdered sugar
2-3 teaspoons milk
1 teaspoon vanilla

Dough: In a mixing bowl, combine warm water with 1 tablespoon sugar. Add the yeast and stir to dissolve. Set aside for 5 minutes. In a medium saucepan, scald the milk, butter, sugar and salt. Remove from the heat and stir in the sour cream.

In a mixing bowl, add the egg yolks and warm milk mixture to the yeast and beat 2 minutes. Add 3 cups of the flour and beat another 2 minutes. Work in the remaining flour to make a soft dough. If the mixer has a dough hook attachment, use it to knead for 7 minutes on medium. If not, turn dough out onto a floured surface and knead until smooth, approximately 10 minutes.

Page sponsored by Dr. Hans Facer, Alpine Dental Care, Martinez 372-7100
In honor of my favorite teacher

Place dough in a lightly oiled bowl turning to coat all sides. Cover loosely with plastic wrap. Place the bowl in an oven that has been preheated to 200° F. and then turned off. Cover with a hot, damp towel. The bowl may be placed in the *dishwasher* which has been turned on for a few minutes and then off, so that there is warm water in the bottom. Close the door and let the dough rise for 45 minutes. The second method may sound strange, but it works well for all types of rising especially pizza dough! Let rise 30-45 minutes.

Filling: Peel, core and dice apples into dime-size pieces. Toss the apples with the lemon zest, juice and sugar. Pour into a large saucepan. Stir and bring to a boil over medium heat. Add the egg yolks. Sprinkle with the flour, cinnamon and stir until thickened, about 3 minutes. Remove from the heat and add the butter, vanilla and walnuts. Let cool to room temperature.

When the dough has risen, punch down and turn out onto a floured surface. Divide it in half and set 1/2 aside. Roll 1/2 into a 10" x 20" rectangle. Spread 1/2 of the apple mixture on top and roll up tightly to create a 20" long roll. Place onto a greased baking sheet seam side down. Shape it into a ring sealing the ends together. Slash the top with a sharp knife every inch, cutting through to the filling. Cover with plastic wrap. Repeat the procedure for the second ring. Let it rise in a warm spot for 30-45 minutes or make the rings the night before, wrap and let them rise in the refrigerator **overnight.** Bring to room temperature before baking.

Preheat oven to 375° F.

Remove plastic wrap and bake for 30 minutes or until light brown.

Glaze: Beat together the cream cheese, powdered sugar, milk and vanilla until smooth. Adjust with milk to achieve desired thickness. When the rings are done, spread the glaze over tops. Slice and enjoy.

Sour Cream Coffee Cake

Cake
1 cup sour cream
1 teaspoon baking soda
1/2 cup butter, softened
1 cup sugar
2 eggs
1 teaspoon vanilla
2 cups flour
1 1/2 teaspoons baking powder

Topping
1/3 cup chopped nuts
1/4 cup sugar
1 teaspoon cinnamon

Preheat oven to 325° F.

Mix the sour cream and baking soda and set aside. Cream the butter and sugar. Blend in the eggs and vanilla Sift the dry ingredients and add to the butter mixture alternating with the sour cream mixture. Mix well after each addition. Pour 1/2 the batter into a greased tube pan. Layer 1/2 of the topping over the batter. Add remaining batter and sprinkle with remaining topping. Bake for 45 minutes.

Serves 10-12.

Page sponsored by the Faculty and Staff of Burton Valley Elementary School

Irish Scones

1 cup self-rising flour
Pinch of salt
1/4 cup sugar
2 teaspoons baking powder
1/4 cup butter
1/4-1/2 cup buttermilk
Milk

Preheat oven to 400° F.

Mix the flour, salt, sugar and baking powder in a bowl. Cut in the butter.
Gradually stir in enough buttermilk to form a soft dough.

On a floured board, roll out the dough to 1/2" thickness. Cut into scones using
a biscuit cutter. Brush with milk. Bake on an ungreased cookie sheet for
15 minutes or until bottoms are lightly browned.

Makes 2 dozen scones.

VARIATION: Currents, orange peel or berries may be added. Approximately
1/4 cup grated cheese may be added if sugar is reduced to 1/8 cup.

Angel Biscuits

1 package dry yeast
1/4 cup warm water
2 cups flour
1 teaspoon salt
1/4 teaspoon baking soda
2 tablespoons sugar
1/4 cup oil
3/4 cup buttermilk

Preheat oven to 425° F.

Dissolve yeast in water and set aside.

Sift together flour, salt, baking soda and sugar. Make a well in the center and add the oil, buttermilk and dissolved yeast, stirring to blend. Add more flour if the batter is too moist.

Turn out onto a floured board and knead for 1-2 minutes. Roll out to a 1" thickness and cut with a biscuit cutter. Place on a greased cookie sheet and let rise for 1/2 hour. If desired, biscuits may be baked without rising.

Bake for 10-12 minutes.

Makes 2 dozen biscuits.

Page sponsored by "The Playgroup"
featuring the Browne, Devor, Fong, Hall, Salzman and Taylor Families

Naan
Indian Yogurt Bread

1 package dry yeast
3/4 cup warm water
3 teaspoons sugar
1/4 cup plain yogurt
1 egg, beaten
1/4 cup melted butter
1 teaspoon salt
3 1/2 cups flour
Melted butter
Poppy seeds

Dissolve the yeast in 1/4 cup warm water. Stir in 1 teaspoon sugar. Let stand until foamy, approximately 10 minutes. Mix the yogurt, remaining sugar, yeast mixture, egg, butter and salt. Stir in 2 cups of the flour and beat until smooth. Add enough flour to make a firm dough.

Knead approximately 10 minutes or until smooth and satiny. Let dough rise in an oiled bowl for at least 1/2 hour or up to 2 hours. Punch down and divide into 8 balls. Let the dough rest for 10 minutes.

Preheat oven to 450° F.

Shape the dough into flat, relatively thin, rounded triangles (approximately 4"-5" per side). Brush with melted butter and sprinkle with poppy seeds. Bake on an ungreased baking sheet until golden, approximately 10 minutes. Serve warm.

NOTE: These are especially good served with Calcutta Curry, page 61.

Herbed Cheese Bread

1 round loaf sourdough French bread
1/2 cup butter
1 tablespoon chopped parsley
1 teaspoon minced onion
1 teaspoon poppy seeds
1/2 pound Monterey Jack cheese, sliced

Preheat oven to 350º F.

Score the loaf into 1 1/2" squares or diamonds, leaving the bottom crust intact. In a small saucepan, melt the butter with the parsley, onion and poppy seeds. Drizzle mixture over the openings in the bread. Insert a cheese slice in each opening. Wrap in foil. The bread may be set aside at this time.

Place on a baking sheet and bake for 15 minutes. Loosen the foil to expose the top and bake another 15 minutes until lightly brown. Serve while hot.

Serves 8.

Mexican Spoon Bread

24 ounces canned cream style corn
3/4 cup milk
1/3 cup melted shortening
2 eggs, slightly beaten
1 cup corn meal
1/2 teaspoon baking soda
1 teaspoon salt
1 cup shredded cheddar cheese
14 ounces canned chopped green chilies

Mix all the ingredients except the cheese and chilies. Pour 1/2 of the batter into a 9" x 9" greased baking dish. Layer with chilies and 1/2 of the cheese. Cover with the remaining batter and sprinkle the top with the remaining cheese.

Bake for 35 minutes. Cool until set.

Serves 12.

Onion Cheese Puffs

1/2 cup butter
1 large onion, chopped
1 cup milk
1 cup flour
4 eggs
1 cup shredded Swiss cheese

Preheat oven to 375º F.

In a frying pan, over medium low heat, melt 1/4 cup of the butter. Add the onion and sauté, stirring frequently. Let cool. In a saucepan, over medium heat, bring the milk and remaining butter to a boil. Add the flour and stir vigorously until the mixture forms a ball. Remove from the heat and beat in the eggs, one at a time, until mixture is smooth. Stir in sautéed onions and 1/2 cup of the cheese.

Spoon 8-12 mounds of dough 2" apart onto a greased cookie sheet. Sprinkle with remaining cheese. Bake in the center of the oven for about 50 minutes. Puffs should be well browned. Serve hot.

NOTE: Cheese puffs may be reheated. They are excellent served at brunch or with soups or stews.

Page sponsored by Lamorinda Veterinary Hospital, Lafayette 284-3636
Paul Bettelheim, D.V.M.

Spinach Feta Crustless Quiche

10 ounces frozen chopped spinach,
   thawed
1/2 cup sliced mushrooms
1 tablespoon butter
6 ounces feta cheese, crumbled
1/2 cup cottage cheese
1 tablespoon vegetable oil
2 cloves garlic, chopped
1 teaspoon basil
1/4 teaspoon oregano
1/4 teaspoon pepper
4 eggs
1/2 cup milk

Preheat oven to 350º F.

Drain and squeeze excess liquid from the spinach. In a frying pan, sauté the mushrooms in butter until soft. In a food processor mix the mushrooms, both cheeses, oil, garlic, basil, oregano and pepper until combined. Add eggs, milk and spinach and process until smooth. Pour into a lightly greased 9" pie plate or 8" square pan.

Bake for 30-40 minutes or until a knife inserted near the center comes out clean. Let stand 5-10 minutes before serving. Serve warm.

Serves 4-6.

NOTE: May be cut into small squares and served as an appetizer.

Page sponsored by The Doré Family - Sheila Valorose, Craig, Ryan and Evan

Breakfast Cheese Strata

12 slices crushed wheat or white bread,
   crusts removed

1/2 pound cooked bacon, Canadian bacon
   or ham, cut into 1/4" strips

2 cups shredded Swiss cheese

6 eggs

3 cups milk

1/2 teaspoon salt

1/8 teaspoon pepper

1 teaspoon dry mustard

1/2 teaspoon marjoram

Generously butter a 9" x 13" baking dish and place 6 slices of the bread on the bottom. Arrange the meat and 1 cup of the cheese over the bread slices. Top with the 6 remaining slices of bread.

In a large bowl, beat the eggs. Add the milk, salt, pepper, dry mustard and marjoram. Pour egg mixture over the bread and top with the remaining cheese. Cover and refrigerate *overnight.*

Preheat oven to 325°F. and bake for 50-55 minutes, until puffed and golden.

Serves 8.

Page sponsored by J. Christopher Thompson, D.D.S., Inc., Walnut Creek 934-3251

Eggs San Juan

Eggs
16 eggs
1 cup sour cream
1 cup milk
Salt and pepper
4 tablespoons butter

Topping
Cheese
Salsa
Green onions
Guacamole
Olives

Preheat oven to 350º F.

Beat the eggs. Add the sour cream, milk, salt and pepper. Melt the butter in a
9" x 13" baking dish. Pour in the egg mixture. Bake approximately 30 minutes
or until set. Sprinkle with toppings and serve.

Page sponsored by Nulaid Foods, in honor of the Ovadia Family

Crab Omelet

From Millie's Kitchen, Lafayette

1 tablespoon butter
3 eggs, beaten
2 slices Monterey Jack cheese
2 ounces crab meat
6 fresh spinach leaves
1 tablespoon chopped green onion

Heat an 8" skillet. Add the butter, tilting the pan to coat bottom and sides. Pour beaten eggs into the skillet and spread to cover the bottom and sides.

Top eggs with cheese, crab, spinach and onions. Cook until eggs are firm and heated. Fold in sides and remove from heat.

—————— ❧ ——————

Trou Pain Perdu

1 stale baguette, sliced into 1" slices
1 1/2 cups milk
4 eggs
1/4 cup orange juice
1/4 cup sugar
Pinch of salt
1 tablespoon vanilla
2 tablespoons Grand Marnier (optional)
Butter
Maple syrup
Fresh fruit

Place the baguette slices in a 9" x 13" baking dish. Whisk together remaining ingredients, except the butter. Pour over the bread and refrigerate for a minimum of 1 hour.

On a griddle, heat the butter until foamy. Remove the bread from the batter and place on the griddle. Turn when golden brown. Toast will be "custardy" but may be cooked longer if preferred. Serve with warmed maple syrup and fresh fruit.

Serves 6.

French Toast Soufflé

16 slices of presliced French bread
16 ounces cream cheese, cubed
12 eggs
2 cups milk
1/2 cup pure maple syrup
Warm maple syrup

Remove the crust and cube the bread. In a 9" x 13" pan, layer 1/2 the bread, the cream cheese, then the remaining bread.

In a bowl, beat the eggs. Add the milk, pure maple syrup and mix well. Pour over all layered ingredients. Cover with plastic wrap and refrigerate **overnight.**

Preheat oven to 375º F.

Bake uncovered for 45 minutes. Cut into squares and serve with warm maple syrup.

Serves 8.

Dutch Apple Pancake

6 tablespoons butter

2 teaspoons cinnamon

1/4 cup sugar

3 large Gravenstein or Granny
   Smith apples, peeled and cored

4 eggs

1 cup flour

1 cup milk

1 1/2 tablespoons powdered sugar

Preheat oven to 425º F.

In a 12" ovenproof frying pan, melt the butter over medium high heat. Stir in the cinnamon and sugar. Thinly slice the apples into the pan. Cook, stirring until the apples are translucent, approximately 5 minutes. Arrange the apples evenly in the pan and place uncovered in the oven for about 5 minutes, while making the batter.

In a blender or food processor, whirl the eggs and flour until smooth. Blend in the milk. Pour the batter evenly over the apples. Bake, uncovered, until the pancake is puffy and golden, about 15 minutes. Dust with powdered sugar and cut into wedges. Serve warm.

Serves 6.

Granola

4 cups rolled oats
1 cup sliced almonds
1/4 cup sesame seeds
1/3 cup brown sugar
1/4 cup vegetable oil
1/4 cup pure maple syrup
1/2 teaspoon cinnamon
1/4 teaspoon vanilla

Preheat oven to 300º F.

Mix the oats, almonds, sesame seeds and brown sugar. In a separate bowl, mix the remaining ingredients. Mix the contents of both bowls together and spread to a 1/2" thickness on an ungreased cookie sheet. Bake for 25 minutes, stirring frequently. Cool. Store in a closed container in the refrigerator.

VARIATION: Nuts, dried fruit, chocolate chips, etc., may be added after granola is cooked and cooled.

Page sponsored by Mr. and Mrs Arthur Laibly
In honor of Ian, Alex and Scott Kidd

DESSERTS

Fudge Fantasy
Apricot Spice Cake
Nonnee's Apple Cake
Marzipan Cake with Berry Sauce
Polish Pound Cake
Quaker Chocolate Cake
Great Plains Cake
Cheesecake
Espresso Cheesecake
Praline Pumpkin Pie
Grandma's Egg Nog Pie
Fresh Fruit Tart
Fruit Cobbler
Peach Rhapsody
Poached Pears with Creme Anglaise
Fruit Sauces
Lemon Creme with Raspberry Sauce
Persimmon Pudding with Lemon Sauce
Mexican Flan
Meringue Torte
Lemon Cream Sorbet
Peppermint Glacier
Frozen Temptation
Sauces for Ice Cream
Country Apple Squares
Black & White Brownies
Chocolate Mint Brownies
Pecan Shortbread

Lemon Shortbread
Chocolate Crescents
Biscotti with Almonds
Chewy Ginger Cookies
Chocolate Crinkles
Persimmon Cookies
Spicy Treasures
Forgotten Cookies
Cookie Monsters
Almond Toffee
Peanut Brittle
Caramel Corn

Fudge Fantasy

Cake
12 ounces semi-sweet chocolate
5 tablespoons espresso or strong coffee
1 cup butter, softened
2 cups sugar
6 egg yolks
1 cup flour
6 egg whites

Glaze
4 ounces bittersweet chocolate
2 tablespoons unsalted butter, melted

Preheat oven to 350° F.

Cake: Grease and flour a 9" springform pan. Combine the semi-sweet chocolate and espresso in a double boiler until the chocolate melts. Remove from the heat and set aside to cool. Cream together the butter and sugar. Add the egg yolks, one at a time, to the creamed mixture. Add the flour. In a medium bowl, beat the egg whites until stiff. Fold the chocolate mixture into the egg whites and then fold into the butter mixture.

Pour the batter into the prepared pan. Bake 60-70 minutes. When done, the top will be crusty and cracked and the middle will still be slightly moist. Cool before glazing.

Glaze: Melt the chocolate in the top of a double boiler over simmering water. Whisk in the melted butter. Pour the glaze over the cake.

VARIATION: You may omit the glaze and dust with powdered sugar.

Page sponsored by Douglas J. Hudson, D.D.S., Orthodontist, Moraga 376-2800

Apricot Spice Cake

Cake

2 cups flour

1 cup sugar

1 1/2 teaspoons cinnamon

1/4 teaspoon allspice

1/4 teaspoon ground cloves

1/2 teaspoon salt

1 heaping teaspoon cornstarch

3 teaspoons cocoa

2 cups canned apricots, drained and chopped

1 cup raisins or chopped dates

1 egg

1 cup chopped nuts

1/2 cup melted shortening

Frosting

12 ounces semi-sweet chocolate

1 cup sour cream

1/4 teaspoon salt

1 teaspoon vanilla

Preheat oven to 350° F.

Cake: Sift together the first 8 ingredients. Add the rest of the ingredients and blend with a mixer. Pour into a greased and floured 9" x 13" pan. Bake for 50-60 minutes.

Frosting: Melt the chocolate in a double boiler over simmering water. Remove from the water and add the remaining ingredients, blending thoroughly. When the cake is cool, frost.

Page sponsored by Joanne Dunne
Pacific Union Residential Brokerage, Lafayette 284-3700

Nonnee's Apple Cake

2 cups apples, diced

1 cup sugar

1 cup flour

1 teaspoon baking soda

1/2 teaspoon salt

3/4 teaspoon baking powder

2 teaspoons cinnamon

1/2 cup vegetable oil

1 egg, beaten

1 teaspoon vanilla

1 cup chopped walnuts

Preheat oven to 350° F.

Place the apples in a large bowl and sprinkle with sugar. Combine the flour, baking soda, salt, baking powder and cinnamon, and sift over the apples. Stir in the oil, egg, vanilla and walnuts. Pour into a greased and floured 9" square pan. Bake 40 minutes.

Marzipan Cake with Berry Sauce

Cake

1/2 cup flour
1/2 teaspoon baking powder
3/4 cup sugar
1/2 cup unsalted butter, softened
8 ounces almond paste

4 eggs
1 tablespoon Muscat Blanc
 or orange liqueur
1/4 teaspoon almond extract
Powdered sugar

Berry Sauce
1 pint fresh berries
2 tablespoons sugar

Preheat oven to 375° F.

Cake: Grease and flour an 8" round cake pan. Cover the bottom of the pan with parchment or wax paper.

Sift the flour and baking powder together and set aside. In a medium bowl, cream the sugar, butter and almond paste. Add one egg at a time. Add the wine and almond extract. Continue beating until the batter triples in size and becomes very light and airy, approximately 5 minutes. Gently fold in the sifted dry ingredients. Do not overmix.

Pour the batter into the prepared cake pan and bake for 40-50 minutes. If the cake is browning too quickly, tent it with foil. When the cake is done, invert it onto a cooling rack. Sift powdered sugar over cooled cake.

Sauce: Purée berries in a food processor or blender. Push the purée through a tight sieve to remove seeds. Add sugar to taste. Ladle a pool of fruit sauce onto a plate and place a slice of marzipan cake on top.

Page sponsored by a Friend of the Cookbook
With warmest thanks to Bill's best friend and her crew

Polish Pound Cake

1 cup butter, softened
2 cups sugar
4 eggs
3 cups flour
1 tablespoon baking powder
1 cup milk
1 tablespoon vanilla
3 ounces bourbon
1 cup chopped nuts
1/3 cup powdered sugar

Preheat oven to 350° F.

Cream butter and sugar until light and fluffy. Add the eggs, one at a time, beating well after each addition. Combine the flour and baking powder. To the creamed mixture alternately add the dry ingredients and the milk. Add the vanilla and bourbon, and fold in 2/3 cup nuts. Pour into a greased tube pan. Sprinkle with a mixture of the powdered sugar and remaining nuts.

Bake for 1 hour. Cool for 5 minutes before removing from the pan.

Quaker Chocolate Cake

1 cup quick oats
1 1/2 cups boiling water
1/2 cup butter
3 eggs
1 1/2 cups flour
1 teaspoon salt
1 teaspoon baking soda
1 tablespoon cocoa
1 cup brown sugar
1 cup sugar
12 ounces mini chocolate chips
3/4 cup chopped nuts

Preheat oven to 350° F.

Mix the oats and water. Let the mixture stand for 10 minutes. Add the butter and eggs. In a separate bowl, sift together flour, salt, baking soda, cocoa and sugars. Add to the wet ingredients. Add 1/2 of the chocolate chips. Pour into a 9" x 13" greased pan. Top with the remaining chocolate chips. Cover with nuts. Bake 45-50 minutes.

Page sponsored by James B. Karol, M.D., Oakland/Alameda 523-0273

Great Plains Cake

Cake

2 cups flour
2 cups sugar
1/2 teaspoon salt
1 cup butter, softened
1 cup water
3 tablespoons cocoa
2 eggs, well beaten
1 teaspoon baking soda
1/2 cup buttermilk
1 teaspoon vanilla

Glaze

1/2 cup butter
3 tablespoons cocoa
6 tablespoons milk
1 box powdered sugar
1 cup chopped nuts
1 teaspoon vanilla

Preheat oven to 350º F.

Cake: Grease and flour a 10" x 15" jelly-roll pan. Sift together the flour, sugar and salt. In a saucepan, combine the butter, water and cocoa, and bring to a boil. Pour over the dry ingredients and mix well. Add the eggs, baking soda, buttermilk and vanilla. Pour into prepared pan. Bake for 20 minutes.

Glaze: While the cake is baking, heat the butter, cocoa and milk in a saucepan. Add the powdered sugar and beat until smooth. Stir in the nuts and vanilla. Pour over the cake while it is still warm. Cool before serving.

Page sponsored by Cape Cod House, Lafayette   283-8288

Cheesecake

Crust
1 1/2 cups graham
    cracker crumbs
6 tablespoons butter
1/4 cup sugar
3/4 teaspoon cinnamon

Cake
32 ounces cream cheese, softened
7 eggs
1 cup sugar
1/8 teaspoon salt
1 1/2 tablespoons lemon juice

Topping
1 teaspoon vanilla
2 cups sour cream
1/4 cup sugar
Kiwi and fresh berries

Preheat oven to 350º F. Place the oven rack in the center of the oven.

Crust: In a food processor, fitted with a steel blade, combine the crust ingredients. Press mixture onto the bottom and cove against the sides of a 9" springform pan. Set aside.

Cake: In the food processor, cream half of the cream cheese and 2 eggs. Add the remaining cream cheese and 2 more eggs. Process. Add the remaining eggs, sugar, salt and lemon juice. Process until thoroughly mixed. Pour into the prepared pan and bake for 45 minutes. Let cool on a wire rack for 15 minutes.

Topping: Increase oven temperature to 475º F. Blend the vanilla, sour cream, and sugar. Spread over the cheese cake and bake for an additional 10 minutes. Remove, cool and refrigerate ***overnight.***

Remove from refrigerator 1 hour before serving and decorate with fresh fruit.

Page sponsored by The Heacock Family and The Sutherland Family

Espresso Cheesecake

Chocolate Crust
24 chocolate wafers
1/4 cup butter, melted
1/4 teaspoon cinnamon

Cheesecake
4 tablespoons freshly ground
   espresso coffee beans
3/4 cup boiling water
24 ounces cream cheese, softened
1 cup sugar
2 eggs
1 cup sour cream
8 ounces semi-sweet chocolate, melted
1 teaspoon vanilla
Chocolate curls or shaved chocolate

Preheat oven to 350º F.

Crust: Using a food processor, crush the chocolate wafers. Mix in the butter and cinnamon. Press into the bottom of a 8" springform pan.

Cake: Place ground coffee in a coffee filter. Pour in boiling water. Measure 1/2 cup of coffee extract and set aside to cool. In a large bowl, beat the cream cheese, sugar and eggs . Blend in the sour cream, melted chocolate, cooled espresso extract and vanilla. Pour into the springform pan and bake for 45 minutes. The center of the cake will be soft. Chill in the refrigerator at least 3 hours or **overnight**. To serve, remove the sides of pan and garnish with chocolate curls or shaved chocolate.

Serves 12.

Praline Pumpkin Pie

Crust - Makes 3 pie shells

4 cups flour

1 teaspoon salt

1 tablespoon sugar

1 3/4 cups shortening

1 tablespoon white vinegar

1 egg

1/2-3/4 cup ice water

Crunchy Praline

1/3 cup unsalted butter

1/3 cup brown sugar

1/2 cup chopped pecans

Filling

1 envelope unflavored gelatin

1/4 cup cold water

3 eggs, separated

1/3 cup sugar

1 1/4 cups cooked, mashed pumpkin

1/2 cup sour cream

1/2 teaspoon salt

1 1/2 teaspoons pumpkin pie spice

1 tablespoon chopped candied ginger

1/4 cup sugar

Preheat oven to 450º F.

Crust: Combine the flour, salt and sugar. Cut in the shortening until crumbly. Mix the vinegar and egg together and add to the flour mixture. Add only as much water as needed to hold dough together. Divide the dough into thirds. Refrigerate 1/3 for 15 minutes. The remaining dough may be frozen for future use.

Roll out the dough to fit into a 9" pie plate. Prick the bottom and sides of the pastry with a fork. Bake 10-12 minutes.

Praline: Reduce oven temperature to 425º F. In a saucepan, combine the butter and brown sugar. Cook, stirring until the sugar melts and mixture bubbles vigorously. Remove from the heat, stir in the pecans and spread over the bottom of the pie shell.

Bake for 5 minutes or until bubbly. Remove from the oven and cool thoroughly.

Page sponsored by Jon E. Sammann, D.D.S., Orthodontics, Lafayette 284-4866

Filling: Soften gelatin in cold water. Beat the egg yolks with 1/3 cup of the sugar. Add the pumpkin, sour cream, salt, spice and ginger. Cook over medium heat, stirring until mixture comes to a boil. Simmer 2 minutes, stirring constantly. Remove from heat and stir in gelatin until dissolved. Cool.

In a bowl, beat egg whites until frothy. Add 1/4 cup sugar and continue to beat until stiff peaks form. Fold the egg whites into the pumpkin mixture. Pour into the praline pie shell and refrigerate. Serve with whipped cream.

Serves 6.

Grandma's Egg Nog Pie

1 9" baked pie shell
   (suggested recipe on page 166)
1 teaspoon unflavored gelatin
1 tablespoon cold water
1 cup milk
1/2 cup sugar
2 tablespoons corn starch
1/4 teaspoon salt
3 egg yolks, lightly beaten
1 tablespoon butter
1 tablespoon vanilla
1 cup heavy cream
Nutmeg for garnish

Combine the gelatin with cold water and set aside. Scald the milk in a double boiler. Combine the sugar, corn starch and salt. Add to the scalded milk and cook, stirring constantly until thickened. Stir a small amount of the hot mixture into the beaten egg yolks. Add yolk mixture to the double boiler and cook 3 minutes. Add the gelatin, butter and vanilla. Cool in the refrigerator.

Whip cream to stiff peaks. Fold whipped cream into cooled filling. Turn into the baked pie shell. Sprinkle with nutmeg and refrigerate until serving.

Serves 6-8.

Page sponsored by Citibank, Lafayette 283-9200

Fresh Fruit Tart

1 prepared 12" tart crust

Filling

3 ounces cream cheese, softened
3/4 cup powdered sugar
1 teaspoon vanilla
1 cup heavy cream, whipped
Fresh fruit such as strawberries, kiwi,
    grapes, peaches, raspberries
    (avoid fresh citrus)

Glaze

1/4 cup sugar
2 1/4 teaspoons cornstarch
1/8 cup orange juice
1 tablespoon lemon juice
1 tablespoon grated lemon rind
1/2 cup water

Preheat oven to 450º F.

Crust: Prepare your favorite 9" double pie crust recipe or use the recipe on page 166. Place dough in a 12" tart pan. Flute edges, prick dough thoroughly and bake for approximately 7-10 minutes.

Filling: Beat the cream cheese. Add the sugar, vanilla and fold in the whipped cream. Spread mixture evenly over baked tart shell. Arrange fresh fruit decoratively on top in concentric circles beginning with the fluted edge and working toward the center. Overlap fruits in order to fully cover the filling.

Glaze: In a saucepan, blend ingredients and stir to dissolve the cornstarch. Simmer over low heat until translucent. Pour over the tart while the glaze is still slightly warm. Refrigerate until ready to serve.

Fruit Cobbler

1/2 cup butter

4 teaspoons baking powder

Pinch of salt

2 cups sugar

2 cups flour

1 1/2 cups milk

8 cups sliced fresh fruit such as:

  apples, peaches, apricots, berries, nectarines

Preheat oven to 350º F.

Melt the butter in a 9" x 13" glass dish. In a bowl, combine the baking powder, salt, sugar, flour and milk. Stir until just moistened. Pour over the melted butter and top with fruit. Bake 40-50 minutes.

Page sponsored by JeNeal and Cal Hatch in honor of Adam and Cody

Peach Rhapsody

Prepare this dessert when peaches are at their peak of perfection. Then pull them out in the dead of winter for a summery treat.

> 6 ripe peaches
> 1 double pie crust recipe
> (suggested recipe on page 166)

Wash and dry the peaches. Divide the pie dough into 6 equal portions. Roll out each portion into a thin circle approximately 8-9" in diameter or large enough to wrap around a peach. Place a peach in the center of each circle and moisten the pastry edges with water. Fold the pastry up around the peach, sealing the edges. Place in a plastic bag and freeze.

Preheat oven to 350º F.

Thaw peaches about 20 minutes, then bake for 1 1/2 hours.

> *Sauce*
> 4 tablespoons butter
> 1 egg
> 1 teaspoon vanilla
> 1/2 teaspoon nutmeg
> 2 cups sifted powdered sugar

Cream together the sauce ingredients and chill. Cool the peaches slightly. Top with sauce and serve with a knife and fork. Yes, there will be a peach pit!

Page sponsored by Barclay Simpson Fine Arts Gallery, Lafayette 284-7048

Poached Pears with Creme Anglaise

Pears

6 pears, Bosc or Anjou,
  slightly underripe
Cold water with lemon juice
1 bottle of champagne or
  dry white wine
1 cup sugar
Juice of 1 lemon
Zest of 1 lemon
1 cinnamon stick
3 whole cloves
2 tablespoons vanilla extract

Creme

1 cup milk
1/2 cup heavy cream
1" piece vanilla bean
6 tablespoons sugar
4 large egg yolks
2 teaspoons cornstarch
2 tablespoons Cognac or
  other liqueur (optional)
Mint leaves

Pears: Peel the pears, leaving the stems. Immerse immediately in lemon water. In a large saucepan, bring all remaining ingredients to a boil and cook for 5 minutes. Lower the heat. Remove the pears from the lemon water and add them to the saucepan. Cook for 20-30 minutes or until pears appear translucent and are easily pierced with a fork. Reserving the liquid, transfer the pears to a shallow dish standing them upright. If necessary, trim the bottoms to make them stand up. Reduce reserved poaching liquid by half. Pour over the pears, cover and chill for several hours.

Creme: In a saucepan, combine the milk, cream and vanilla bean. Bring to a boil, remove from heat and let stand 10 minutes. Remove and discard the bean. In a mixing bowl, gradually add the sugar to the egg yolks. Beat for 3 minutes or until mixture is pale yellow and creamy. Beat in the cornstarch. Using a wire whisk, slowly add the warm cream mixture to the yolks. Beat vigorously. Return mixture to the saucepan and cook over very low heat, stirring constantly with a wooden spoon until the mixture is quite thick and coats the back of the spoon, approximately 15 minutes. Do not let it boil. Remove from the heat, stir in liqueur, if desired, and cool, stirring frequently. Cover and chill thoroughly.

Spoon a thin layer of sauce onto the bottom of a dessert plate. Stand the pear in the center and garnish with mint leaf.

VARIATION: Semi-sweet chocolate may be melted and drizzled over the pear before serving.

Fruit Sauces

Two sauces to enhance the natural glory of fresh summer fruits.

Jamaican Rum Sauce

1 1/2 cup sour cream

1/4 cup brown sugar

1 tablespoon white rum

1 tablespoon whiskey

1/4 cup raisins

Combine all ingredients except the raisins and whisk until smooth. Blend in the raisins. Cover and refrigerate at least 2 hours.

Loaded Lemon Sauce

1/2 cup heavy cream

1/2 cup sour cream

1-2 tablespoons sugar

Juice of 1/2 lemon

1/2-1 jigger vodka

Mint leaves

Mix cream, sour cream and sugar. Add the lemon juice, stirring constantly to avoid curdling the sour cream. Blend in the vodka. Garnish with mint leaves.

Page sponsored by Kenneth Sutherland Co., Oakland 893-0772
In honor of Katie and Kristina Sutherland

Lemon Creme with Raspberry Sauce

Creme

1 cup sugar
2 tablespoons cornstarch
1/4 teaspoon salt
1 cup water
1/4 cup fresh lemon juice
1 egg yolk, lightly beaten
1 teaspoon grated lemon rind
1 teaspoon vanilla
1 cup heavy cream
Sprigs of mint

Sauce

10 ounces frozen sweetened
   raspberries, thawed
1/4 cup sugar
1 1/2 teaspoons cornstarch
2 tablespoons water

Creme: In a saucepan combine the sugar, cornstarch and salt. Gradually stir in the water. Cook over medium heat, stirring constantly until the mixture thickens.

Combine the lemon juice and egg yolk and stir into the hot mixture. Bring to a slow boil and cook 1 minute. Cool mixture, stirring occasionally to prevent the formation of a skin. Add the lemon rind and vanilla. Chill. This can be prepared up to 1 day in advance.

Sauce: Place the raspberries in a small saucepan and crush with a potato masher. Add sugar and simmer 5 minutes or until sugar is completely dissolved. Mix the cornstarch and water and add to the berries. Simmer 5 minutes stirring constantly. Chill.

When ready to serve, whip the cream and fold into the chilled lemon mixture. Spoon into dessert bowls and top with sauce. Garnish with a mint leaf.

Persimmon Pudding with Lemon Sauce

Pudding
1 cup persimmon pulp
2 teaspoons baking soda
1/2 cup butter, softened
1 1/2 cups sugar
2 eggs
1 teaspoon lemon juice
2 teaspoons vanilla
4 teaspoons brandy
1 cup flour
1 teaspoon cinnamon
1/2 teaspoon salt
1 cup golden raisins
1/2 cup chopped pecans

Sauce
2/3 cup sugar
2 tablespoons cornstarch
1/2 teaspoon salt
1/3 cup lemon juice
1 cup water
1 cup heavy cream, whipped

Preheat oven to 350° F.

Pudding: In a bowl, combine the persimmon pulp and baking soda and set aside. Cream the butter and sugar until fluffy. Beat in eggs, one at a time. Add the lemon juice, vanilla and brandy. Stir in the persimmon pulp mixture. Stir in the dry ingredients and add raisins and nuts.

Pour into a greased bundt pan. Place the filled pan into a 9" x 13" baking pan and put both into the oven. Add water to fill the baking pan half way. Bake for 2 1/2 hours. Cool for 10 minutes. Serve with Lemon Sauce.

Sauce: Cook the sugar, cornstarch, salt, lemon juice and water over moderate heat, stirring constantly until clear and thickened. Cool. Fold in the whipped cream and blend well.

Page sponsored by Desco Plaza Office Center, Lafayette 283-8470

Mexican Flan

1 cup sugar

1- 14 ounce can of Eaglebrand
   sweetened condensed milk

1- 12 ounce can evaporated milk

Whole milk, to fill the Eaglebrand can

4 eggs

1 tablespoon vanilla

Preheat oven to 350º F.

On the bottom rack of the oven place a large flat metal pan containing 1/2" of warm water. This pan must to be large enough to accomodate a 9 1/2" round dish.

In a saucepan, over medium low heat, melt the sugar, stirring with a wooden spoon until dissolved. Pour the melted sugar into a 9 1/2" round glass dish and using a wooden spoon, spread the sugar on the bottom and sides before it hardens. Work quickly! As the sugar hardens, it should have a crackly appearance.

In a blender, combine the milks, eggs and vanilla. Pour 1/2 of this mixture into the glazed dish. Set the dish into the pan of water which has been warming in the oven. Pour the remaining 1/2 of the mixture into the pie dish. The dish will now be very full. Slide it carefully into the oven and bake for 1 hour or until a knife, when inserted in the center, comes out clean.

Cool on a wire rack at room temperature. Cover the dish with a serving plate and invert. This is best served at room temperature.

Page sponsored by California Savings & Loan, A.F.A., Branches in Lafayette and Moraga

Meringue Torte

6 egg whites
2 teaspoons vanilla
1/2 teaspoon cream of tartar
2 cups sugar
6 Heath candy bars,
   3/4 ounce size, frozen
2 cups heavy cream, whipped

Preheat oven to 275° F.

Cover two cookie sheets with brown paper and draw a 9" circle on each.

Beat the egg whites, vanilla and cream of tartar to soft peaks. Gradually beat in the sugar until very stiff peaks form. Spread the meringue on the paper, within the lines using a spatula or pastry bag.

Bake for 1 hour. Turn off the heat and let dry for at least 2 hours in the closed oven.

Crush the Heath bars, reserving some for garnish. Fold the remaining candy gently into the whipped cream. Place one meringue round on a serving platter and spread 1/2 the whipped cream mixture on top. Place the second circle on top and spread with remaining mixture. Garnish with reserved crushed candy and chill *overnight.*

Serves 12.

Page sponsored by Foley, McIntosh & Foley, Attorneys-at-Law, Lafayette 284-3020

Lemon Cream Sorbet

3/4 cup sugar
1/2 cup fresh lemon juice
Grated rind of 2 lemons
2 cups heavy cream
2 cups fresh berries

In a small bowl, combine the sugar and lemon juice. Stir until the sugar is dissolved. Add the lemon rind and cream. Pour into an 8" x 4" metal loaf pan. Freeze until firm, approximately 3-4 hours. Let stand at room temperature 10-15 minutes before serving. Scoop into parfait dishes and top with fresh berries.

Peppermint Glacier

1/4 cup sugar
1/2 cup butter, melted
1 1/4 cup crushed chocolate wafers
  (approximately 24)
8 ounces cream cheese, softened
14 ounces sweetened condensed milk
2 cups whipping cream
1 cup crushed peppermint candy
Whipped cream

Combine the sugar, butter and chocolate wafer crumbs in a bowl. Press into the bottom of a 10" springform pan. Place in the refrigerator while preparing the filling.

Beat the cream cheese until fluffy. Add the condensed milk and beat until well blended. In a bowl, whip the cream to stiff peaks and fold into the cream cheese mixture. Gently fold in crushed candy and pour onto the crust. Cover with plastic wrap and freeze overnight. Place in the refrigerator for a few hours before serving.

Remove pie from springform pan. Garnish with whipped cream, if desired.

Frozen Temptation

2 packages of lady fingers
1 pint chocolate chip ice cream, softened
12 ounces caramel sauce
1/2 pound toffee candy, crushed
1 pint coffee ice cream, softened
12 ounces chocolate sauce

Line the sides and bottom of a 9" springform pan with lady fingers. Spread with chocolate chip ice cream. Cover with caramel sauce and 1/2 of the toffee candy. Spread the coffee ice cream on top and cover with chocolate sauce. Top with the remaining toffee candy. Freeze **overnight.** Remove from springform pan, slice and serve.

NOTE: This recipe can be made 3-5 days ahead.

Sauces for Ice Cream

Chocolate Cinnamon Sauce

1 pound semi-sweet chocolate chips

1/2 cup butter

1/2 cup milk

1/2 cup heavy cream

1 1/2 teaspoons cinnamon

1/4 cup bourbon

Cinnamon

In the top of a double boiler, over simmering water, melt the chocolate and butter. In a heavy saucepan, over medium heat, scald the milk and cream with the cinnamon. Gradually stir in the chocolate mixture. Blend in the bourbon. Stir in additional cinnamon to taste.

Hot Fudge Sauce

1/2 cup heavy cream

3 tablespoons sweet butter, cut into small pieces

1/3 cup granulated sugar

1/3 cup dark brown sugar

Pinch of salt

1/2 cup Dutch-process cocoa powder

In a saucepan, over moderate heat, combine the cream and the butter. Stir until the butter is melted and mixture comes to a slow boil. Add both sugars, stirring until dissolved. Reduce the heat, add salt and cocoa and stir briskly with a small wire whisk until smooth.

Page sponsored by Floral Arts Florist, Lafayette 284-5765
Sally and Chuck Houston

Country Apple Squares

Dough
2 cups flour
1/2 cup sugar
1/2 teaspoon baking powder
1/2 teaspoon salt
1 cup butter
2 egg yolks, beaten

Filling
1/3 cup sugar
1/4 cup flour
1 teaspoon cinnamon
6-7 apples, peeled, cored
 and thinly sliced
Powdered sugar

Preheat oven to 350º F.

Dough: Combine the flour, sugar, baking powder and salt. Cut in the butter until the mixture is crumbly. Stir in the egg yolks. Press 1/2 of the mixture into a 9" x 13" pan. Bake for 10-12 minutes.

Filling: In a bowl mix the sugar, flour and cinnamon. Combine the apples and sugar mixture and layer over bottom crust. Crumble the remaining dough over the apples. Bake for 35 minutes. Cool, then sprinkle with powdered sugar.

NOTE: These are excellent served in large squares and topped with French Vanilla Ice Cream.

Page sponsored by Elite Tile, Walnut Creek 932-4101

Black & White Brownies

Chocolate Batter

1 cup flour

1 teaspoon baking powder

1/2 teaspoon salt

8 ounces semi-sweet chocolate

6 tablespoons butter

4 eggs

1 1/2 cups sugar

2 teaspoons vanilla

2 cups walnuts, chopped

Cheese Batter

8 ounces cream cheese,
  softened

4 tablespoons butter

1 teaspoon vanilla

1/2 cup sugar

2 eggs

Preheat oven to 350º F.

Chocolate Batter: Mix the flour, baking powder and salt. Melt the chocolate and butter in a double boiler. Cool slightly. In a separate bowl, beat the eggs, sugar and vanilla. Add the chocolate mixture and mix well. Add the flour mixture a little at a time, blending well between each addition. Set aside one cup of this batter. Add 1 cup walnuts to the remaining batter.

Cheese Batter: In a medium bowl, combine all the cheese batter ingredients.

Grease and flour a 9" x 13" baking pan. Pour the chocolate & walnut batter into the prepared pan, followed by the cheese batter. Top with the reserved chocolate batter and the remaining walnuts.

Bake 35 minutes.

Page sponsored by East Bay Pediatrics, Berkeley 841-5383 and Orinda 254-9203

Chocolate Mint Brownies

Brownies
2 squares bittersweet chocolate
1/2 cup butter
2 eggs
1 cup sugar
1/2 cup flour
1/4 teaspoon salt
1/4 teaspoon peppermint extract
1/3 cup chopped nuts

Filling
1 cup powdered sugar
1 tablespoon heavy cream
3/4 teaspoon peppermint extract
2 tablespoons butter

Glaze
1 square bittersweet chocolate
1 tablespoon butter

Preheat oven to 350º F.

Grease and flour a 9" square baking pan.

Brownies: Melt the chocolate and butter in a double boiler. In a bowl, beat the eggs until frothy. Add the chocolate mixture and sugar and mix well. Add remaining ingredients and pour into prepared pan. Bake 20-25 minutes. Cool.

Filling: Mix all ingredients and spread over the top of the cooled brownies. Place in the refrigerator for 1/2 hour.

Glaze: Melt ingredients together and stir to blend. Drizzle over filling.

Cool before cutting.

Page sponsored by Stanley Intermediate School P.T.A.

Pecan Shortbread

2/3 cup unsalted butter
1/2 cup light brown sugar
1 teaspoon vanilla
1 1/2 cups flour
1 cup finely chopped pecans
Sugar
Raw Sugar

Preheat oven to 325º F.

Beat the butter and brown sugar until fluffy. Add the vanilla. Combine the flour and nuts and add to the mixture in fourths, beating well after each addition.

On a flat surface, sprinkled with granulated sugar, roll dough out to 3/8" thickness. Cut with a small biscuit or cookie cutter. Sprinkle the topside of the cookie with raw sugar. Bake 14 minutes on a greased cookie sheet.

Makes 2 dozen.

Lemon Shortbread

3/4 cup butter, softened
1/2 cup powdered sugar
1 1/2 cups flour
1/4 teaspoon salt
1/2 teaspoon vanilla
2 tablespoons grated lemon zest
2 tablespoons sugar

Cream the butter and powdered sugar until light and fluffy. In a separate bowl, sift together the flour and salt and add to butter mixture. Add the vanilla and lemon zest and blend thoroughly. Gather into a ball and wrap in plastic wrap. Refrigerate 4-6 hours.

Remove from the refrigerator and allow to soften slightly. Press into an 8" square pan. Score dough into 16 portions. Sprinkle with sugar and refrigerate uncovered for 45 minutes.

Preheat oven to 325° F.

Bake until the shortbread is starting to color slightly, approximately 20 minutes. Cool. Cut shortbread into 16 bars.

Page sponsored by The John Robinson Family

Chocolate Crescents

Cookie
3 1/2 cups flour
1 teaspoon baking powder
1 cup butter, softened
8 ounces cream cheese, softened
2 cups sugar
1 egg
1 teaspoon vanilla
12 ounces miniature semi-sweet
   chocolate chips

Glaze
6 ounces semi-sweet chocolate chips
2 tablespoons shortening

Preheat oven to 375° F.

Cookie: In a medium bowl, stir together the flour and baking powder. Set aside. In a large mixing bowl, beat the butter and cream cheese. Add the sugar and beat until fluffy. Beat in egg and vanilla. Gradually blend in the flour mixture. Fold in the mini chips.

Shape rounded teaspoons of dough into 2"logs. Place on an ungreased cookie sheet. Bend and pinch the ends to form a crescent. Bake for 8-10 minutes or until edges are firm and bottoms are a light golden brown. Cool on a wire rack.

Glaze: In a heavy saucepan, melt the chocolate and shortening. Dip one end of the cooled crescents into the glaze. Lay the cookie on wax paper until the chocolate is set.

Biscotti with Almonds

These are Italian dipping cookies with a hard, dense texture. For full flavor, dip into coffee, red wine or hot chocolate.

2 cups flour

1 cup sugar

1 teaspoon baking powder

1 1/2 teaspoons anise seed

3 eggs

2 tablespoons grappa*

2 tablespoons Frangelico*

1 teaspoon vanilla

1 teaspoon anise extract

1 teaspoon almond extract

1 1/2 cups whole or sliced almonds

Preheat oven to 300º F.

Grease and flour a large baking sheet.

Mix the flour, sugar, baking powder and anise seed. Set aside. In a separate bowl, beat the eggs and add the remaining liquid ingredients. Combine with the dry ingredients and mix until well blended. Add the almonds and mix gently. Turn batter, which will be sticky, onto the baking sheet and form into a long loaf approximately 5" wide and 1/2" to 1" high.

Bake for approximately 50 minutes until the loaf is firm and dry. Remove from the baking sheet and cool 10 minutes. Slice into 1/2" slices and return to the baking sheet, cut side down. Bake 25 minutes. Turn cookies over and bake for an additional 25 minutes. Cookies should appear "toasted". Cool completely.

*Available at liquor stores.

Chewy Ginger Cookies

3/4 cup butter

1 cup sugar

1 egg

4 tablespoons Grandma's Molasses

2 cups flour

1 teaspoon cinnamon

1 1/4 teaspoons ground ginger

1/2 teaspoon ground cloves

1 teaspoon baking soda

Raw sugar

Cream together the butter and sugar until fluffy. Add the egg and molasses. Mix together all remaining ingredients except the raw sugar and add to the creamed mixture. Refrigerate dough 1 to 1 1/2 hours.

Preheat oven to 350º F.

Shape dough into 1" balls and roll in raw sugar. Place them 2" apart on a greased cookie sheet. Bake for 10-12 minutes. Do not overbake. They come out soft but firm up when cooled.

Makes 2-3 dozen.

Page sponsored by Chroma Industries, Lafayette, Ralph P. Boghosian
In honor of Lindsay and Kacie Sturman

Chocolate Crinkles

1 cup semi-sweet chocolate chips
1 cup brown sugar
1/3 cup vegetable oil
2 eggs
1 teaspoon vanilla
1 cup flour
1 teaspoon baking powder
1/4 teaspoon salt
1/2 cup chopped walnuts
1/2 cup powdered sugar

Preheat oven to 350º F.

Melt the chocolate and combine with the sugar and oil. Beat in the eggs, one at a time and add the vanilla. Combine the flour, baking powder and salt and add to the chocolate mixture. Stir in the nuts. Chill the dough.

Drop by teaspoonfuls into powdered sugar, roll to coat and place on a greased cookie sheet. Bake for 10 minutes.

Makes 4 dozen.

Page sponsored by Vicki Englert, Residential Real Estate Specialist
Pacific Union Residential Brokerage, Lafayette 284-3700

Persimmon Cookies

1 cup sugar
1/2 cup shortening
1 cup persimmon pulp
1 teaspoon baking soda
1 egg, beaten
2 cups flour
1 teaspoon cinnamon
1/2 teaspoon cloves
1/2 teaspoon salt
1 cup chopped nuts
1 cup raisins

Preheat oven to 375° F.

Cream the sugar and shortening. Add the persimmon pulp and baking soda, mixing well. Blend in the remaining ingredients. Drop by rounded teaspoonfuls onto a greased baking sheet.

Bake for 12-15 minutes.

Makes 3 dozen.

Page sponsored by a Friend of the Cookbook as a tribute to Dennis Begg

Spicy Treasures

1/2 cup butter

1/2 cup shortening

1 cup brown sugar

1 cup sugar

1 1/2 teaspoons vanilla

2 eggs

3 teaspoons cinnamon

1 teaspoon nutmeg

1 teaspoon mace

2 teaspoons ground cloves

1 1/2 cups flour

1 1/4 teaspoons baking soda

1 teaspoon salt

1 cup walnuts, chopped

1 cup Rice Krispies

1 cup unsweetened coconut

2 cups rolled oats

12 ounces chocolate chips

Preheat oven to 350° F.

Cream the butter, shortening, sugars, vanilla, eggs and spices together. Add the flour, baking soda, salt and mix well. Stir in remaining ingredients. Drop by tablespoonfuls onto greased cookie sheets.

Bake 8-10 minutes.

Makes 7-8 dozen.

Page sponsored by Roughing It Day Camp for children age 3-16, Lafayette 283-3795

Forgotten Cookies

2 egg whites
3/4 cup sugar
1 teaspoon vanilla
1/4 teaspoon salt
1 cup broken pecans
1 cup chocolate chips

Preheat oven to 350º F.

Line 2 cookie sheets with foil.

Beat the egg whites until peaks begin to form. Add the sugar, one tablespoon at a time. Add the vanilla and salt. Continue to beat until stiff and shiny. Fold in the pecans and chocolate chips. Drop by teaspoonfuls onto the cookie sheets. Place in the oven. Turn off the oven and leave the cookies in the oven *overnight.* In the morning, remove cookies and store in air tight containers.

Makes 4-6 dozen cookies.

Cookie Monsters

1 cup margarine, softened

1 pound brown sugar

2 cups sugar

6 eggs

1/2 tablespoon light corn syrup

2 teaspoons vanilla

1 1/2 pounds peanut butter

4 teaspoons baking soda

9 cups rolled oats

3/4 pound chocolate chips

3/4 pound M & M's

Preheat oven to 375° F.

Cream together the margarine, sugars, eggs, syrup, vanilla and peanut butter. Add the baking soda, rolled oats, chocolate chips and M & M's. Scoop with an ice cream server onto a greased cookie sheet and flatten slightly. Bake for 12 minutes.

Makes 4 dozen.

Almond Toffee

1 pound butter

1 cup brown sugar

1 cup sugar

12 ounces semi-sweet chocolate chips

1 1/2 cups almonds, finely chopped

Line a 12" x 18" pan with foil. Combine the butter and sugars in a medium saucepan. Cook over medium heat, stirring constantly until mixture reaches the hard crack stage (310° F. on a candy thermometer).

Pour the mixture onto the foiled pan. Spread quickly but do not stir. Scatter 1/2 of the chocolate chips over the top. As the chocolate melts, spread it to cover the surface completely. Pat on 1/2 of the almonds. Cool in the refrigerator 25 minutes.

Turn the mixture out of the pan and remove foil. Melt remaining chocolate and spread over the toffee mixture. Pat on the remaining nuts. Chill until firm. Cut or break into chunks using the point of a sharp knife.

Peanut Brittle

1 cup sugar
1/2 cup light corn syrup
1 cup roasted, salted peanuts
1 teaspoon butter
1 teaspoon vanilla
1 teaspoon baking soda

Lightly grease one cookie sheet.

In a 2 quart microwaveable bowl, combine the sugar and syrup. Microwave on high 4 minutes. Stir in peanuts. Microwave on high 3-5 minutes until light brown. Add the butter and vanilla, blending well. Microwave on high an additional 1-2 minutes. Add the baking soda and stir until light and foamy. Spread onto the prepared cookie sheet. Cool 1/2 hour. Break into pieces.

Makes 1 pound of candy.

Caramel Corn

1 cup butter
1 cup brown sugar
1/4 cup corn syrup
1/2 teaspoon salt
1/2 teaspoon vanilla
1/4 teaspoon baking soda
3 quarts popped popcorn,
approximately 1 cup kernels

Preheat oven to 350º F.

In a medium saucepan, combine the butter, brown sugar, syrup and salt. Bring to a boil, stirring constantly. Reduce the heat and boil for 5 minutes undisturbed. Remove from the heat and quickly stir in the vanilla and baking soda. Combine with the popcorn and place in a roasting pan. Bake 1 hour, stirring every 15 minutes. Cool 1 hour. Break into pieces and store in an airtight container.

VARIATION: Peanuts, walnuts or almonds may be added.

*F*or their financial support in making *The Lafayette Collection* a reality, we thank the businesses and individuals listed on the honor rolls that follow:

Business Honor Roll

Avalon Bay Foods

Arrow Travel, Lafayette

Bank of America, Lafayette

Better Homes Realty, Lafayette

Brooks & Beaver Insurance
  Agency, Inc., Lafayette

California School Employees
  Association, Lafayette

Campana Music, Lafayette

The Cotton Patch, Lafayette

Friend of the Cookbook

Dossey Chiropractic, Lafayette

Encore Gymnastics, Walnut Creek

Face to Face, Lafayette

Fastframe Custom Framing, Lafayette

Flavio's, Lafayette

Fumble Fingers, Lafayette

Gold N' Goodies, Lafayette

Govan Associates - Architecture,
  Walnut Creek

Hair Studio 3322, Lafayette

Harriet Plummer Aquatic School,
  Lafayette

HDO Architects/Planners,
  Walnut Creek

Johnny's Donut Shop, Lafayette

Kumon Math Center, Walnut Creek

Lafayette Garden Club, Lafayette

Lafayette Health Club, Lafayette

Lafayette Sewing Center, Lafayette

Lafayette 76, Lafayette

Levin & Menzies, Inc., Emeryville

Mail Boxes Etc., Lafayette

Matsutani & Company, Inc., Concord

Jacksons Wines and Spirits, Lafayette

Mortgage Advantage, Walnut Creek

Mt. Diablo Veterinary Medical
  Center, Inc., Lafayette

Oak Creek Dental Office, Pleasant Hill

Pediatrics, Pleasant Hill

Ronald Hufft, Attorney at Law,
  Walnut Creek

Sanwa Bank California

The Squirrels Coffee Shop, Lafayette

Stephen Stanley Graphic Design, Lafayette

Handlebar Toys, Lafayette

The Sweat Shop, Lafayette

Tobin & Tobin, Attorneys at Law,
  Walnut Creek

Togo's Eatery, Lafayette

Traverso Tree Service, Walnut Creek

Village Tours & Travel, Orinda

Family Honor Roll

Khaled, Synneve Alameddine & Family
The Albert Family
The Alvarez Family
The Anders Family
Mike, Marilyn, Kirsten,
   Eric & Hilary Andersen
Marty, Karen, Kristofer &
   Stacy Anderson
Royce Anderson & Family
Sascha, Zane & Trevor Anderson
James, Andrew, Carol &
   Terry Applebury
Wes, Joanne, Mary Jane, John,
   Suzanne & Curtis Ashford
The Balestrieri Family
The Barber-Macbride Family
Diane, Jon, Beth, Jenny, Holly &
   Emily Barbera
David & Kathy Barleen & Family
The Gary Beeler Family
The Benoit Family
Phillip, Michele & Matthew Berry
The David Besenfelder Family
Craig Bigelow, Jackie Hopkins-Bigelow
   & Daniel Hopkins
Bob, Nancy, Justin & Tim Bishop
Howard & Heidi Bishop & Family
Tom, Debbie Wiley, Erin &
   Eugene Bishop
Richard, Donna, Alycia & Alex Black
Candice, Steven, Zach & Zane
   Blackman

Rich, Denise & Brendan Blakewell
The Blazick Family
Robert, Marie & Matthew Blits
The Block Family
Lorin, Ivy, Nicole, Amy & Tyler Blum
Rick & Kathy Bowles
Rodger, Donna & Lyndsey Brackley
Mark, Kim, Daniel & Christine Brast
Mark, Kathy, Mallory & Dana Bressler
The Brondello Family
Jeff Brush & Family
Rick, Ginny, Joe and Ted Bruzzone
Jerry & Marilyn Burke
Pattie, Glen, Ariane & Claire Buser
Andy, Brianne & Brendan Byrne
M. Ian & Janet Callow
Ken, Chris & Billy Cameron
Jennifer Campbell's Family
Bill, Susan, Melissa & Mac Caplan
The Careys
Steve, Judy, Matt & Johanna Carney
The Cartmell-Martins
The Chandler Family
Elmer, Paulette, Kathryn &
   Carolyn Chinn
Jun, Eun & Woo Cho
Wymond & Terry Choy
Mr. & Mrs. Barry Christensen &
   Children
The Chung Family
Susan Gabriel and Justin & Jessica Clark
Zach & Sam Clark

Tom, Kathy, BJ & Diana Clausen
The Coakley Family
Mike, Betty, Eric & David Coan
Irwin, Judith & Darrin Cohen
Joe & Marianne Coleman
The Colletts
Peter, Margo, Joshua, Brian &
    Zack Connolly
Laura Cooper & her Mom,
    Dad & Sister
Conrad, Elizabeth, Michael,
    Melanie & Gregory Corbett
Ken and Emile Corcoran & Family
The Cotter's
Kay Countryman
Mr. & Mrs. John Cox & Family
The Crawfords
The Croft Family
Cathy & Dee Cullom
Christine & Jim Cunha & Family
Tom, Wynnae, Taylor &
    Channing Dahl
Kae, Pam, Marc, Matthew &
    Gregg Davidson
Joe, Sue, Jenny, Lauren &
    Tom DeGirolamo
George, Joan, Brud, Rhea &
    Jason Denny
Jeff, Melinda, Elise, Laura &
    Marie Dieden
The Diemer Family

The Family of Zachary &
    Jenna Diestler
Mike & Sharon Dixon & Family
Carl, Pat, Beth & Michelle Doughty
The Dove Family
Marty & Gail Drexler & Family
Joe & Juana Droessler
Bill, Valerie & Alex Duncan
John, Charlie, Matt & Chris
    Eaton & Beth Ferree
The Ebe Family
Mom, Dad & Danny Ebert
The Jack Edelen Family
The David Edwards Family
Janey and Michael Edwards
Bill, Reneé, Jason & John Egan
The Ehret Family
Mary, Michael, Rachel & Zach
    Eilerman/Messer
John and Pam Elliott
Lance, Trudy and Jordan Engeldinger
The Enna Family
Steve, Rhondda, Stephen &
    Brian Etheredge
Glenn, Tracey, Caitlin,
    Shannon & Devon Farrell
The Felt Family
Crystal, Andrew, Joan & Alan Fernandes
Gordon, Penny, Kaitlin & Kevin Fickle
Marty, Sally, Laura & Stephanie Fischer
Bill & Cindy Fisher, Valerie &
    Diana Johnson

Debbie, Alan, Darcie &
  Alison Flansburg
The Flynnperrault Family
The Andersson Fogel Family
George, Chris, Eric & Matthew Fong
The Forenza Family
Vince, Amy, Tony, Marisa &
  Gina Forte
Brett, Marguerite & Christine Foster
The Foy Family
Denise France & Breanna Cunningham
Jerry, Greta, Megan & Jonathan Frantz
Friend of the Cookbook
Friend of the Cookbook
Friend of the Cookbook
Friend of the Cookbook
Friend of the Cookbook
Friend of the Cookbook
Friend of the Cookbook
Friend of the Cookbook
Friend of the Cookbook
The Fujimori-Smith Family
Bruce, Eda, Scott, Justin &
  Brian Fukayama
Jerry, Gail & Alene Gabriel
The Galer Family
John, Sue, Christopher, Lindsey,
  Devin & Alexander Gallo
Geoff, Judy, Chris, Matt &
  Sander Garden
The Garretts

Steve & Sue George & Family
The Gilman Family
The Robert Gingery Family
Miriam, Norm, Jeff & Sam Glickman
Bonnie, Mitchell, Aaron &
  Shana Godfred
Nicholas Gold & Family
Dennis, Janet, Eric & Mark Govan
The Graffis Family
The Greer Family
Susan, John Michael & Philip Gyulai
Joe, Kate, Erin & Ryan Hafey
Brian, Terese & Maria Hagerty
Houman, Hedieh, Ali &
  Marzieh Haghighi
The Hansen Family
The Hardin Family
Jack, Barbara, Danny & Katie Harkins
The Harmon Family
Jenny, Jeffrey, Jan & Ted Harms
Jamie, Martha, Jonathan,
  Sarah & Benjamin Harris
The Richard T. Harris Family
Sue, Dave, Matt & Ben Hartman
Amanda Harvey
Harry, Sharon & Bradley Hasegawa
Mike & Marsha Haverty
Rick, Marcia, Rebecca & Scott Hazard
Tom, Lois, Michael &
  Matthew Henderson
Ken & Kris Hertel

Linda, Larry, Jon, Andrew &
    Lexi Hill
Morris & Mae Ho
Kevin, Eddy, Emily & Jake Hoffberg
Bill & Janet Hoffman & Family
Mark, Susan, Annie &
    Drew Hoffman
Brian, Danny & Ricky Holligan
The Honeyman Family
The Horan Family
Steve, Jane, Kate & Britt Howe
The Howekamp Family
Ron, Jane, Amy & Brian Hufft
Terri & Rick Humann
The Hunt Family
Bob & Kathy Hunter & Tanner Burke
The Imbellinos
Brendan, Devin & Galen Jackson
Stan, Naomi, Sara & Darren Jacobs
Ron & Janet Zuzack, Keith &
    Kortney Jamtaas
The Jenkins-Stark Family
George, Marion, Hilary, Tyler &
    Marsall Johnson
Molly, Travis, Brad & Linda Jones
Greg, Jean, Robyn & Philip Jones
The Jorgensen Family
The Ken Kaplan Family
Jim, Kathy, Jenny & David Karol
The Karsant Family
The Katibah Family

Neil & Diane Kelly & Family
Lonna, Brianne & Shauna Kennedy
Karla Kiefert
Shirley Siegel & Walter Kieser
The Family of Sumi & Steven Kim
Eric, Deborah, Jennifer and
    Jeffrey Kolhede
The Kolman-Leland Family
Herb, Kathy, Nicole & Lila Korpell
The Kostka Family
The Krikorians
The Lake Family
David & Lena Lamel
The Landstra Family
Daniel, Beverly, Allison, Scott &
    Bret Lathrope
William, Diane, Justin & Cody Lee
Marty, Don, Chris & Justin Lenzi
Ellen B. Lev & Children
The Lewis Family
The Lowenstein Family
The Lussing-Otten Family
The Lyle Family
Dave & Patty Machado
The Maddux Family
Gil & Peggy Magilen
The Mahl Family
David Mancherje & Family
Gene & Mary Mannee
The Marienthal Family
Bob, Kathlyn, Jesse & Jenna Martin

Karin Massey
The Massies
David, Lita, Greg & Ryan Mathy
Peter, Sonja, Sophia & Susannah Maund
Karen Mazanis
The McFadden Family
The McKnight Family
Phillip, Beverly Lateef, Stephanie & Jennifer McLeod
The McLin Family
Sally, Bob, Melissa & Molly Mehaffey
Jack, Marianne, John & Rob Meinbress
Laura, Collin, Ryan & Andrew Melton
Gene, Robin & Jonathan Menzies
Leigh, Chris, Geoff & Val Meredith
Dick & Laurie Miles
The Miller Family
Len, Marie, Jessica, Jordan & Cecily Miller
The Steve Miller Family
The Mohanta Family
The Mollett Family
Andrew & JoAnn Morse
The Moskowitz Family
Mr. & Mrs. Toyohiko Muraki & Family
Jim, Frankie, Brennan & Emily Murray
Terry, Linda, Megan & Lauren Murray
Ron, Mary, Betsy & Emily Nahas
Dan, Susan, Shannon & Ryan Navarro
The Nayak Family
Bruce, Noelle, Steven & Sarah Neighbor
Doug, Nancy, David & Melanie Nelson

The Nisen Family
The Noceti Family
The Nunes Family
The O'Brien Family
Megan & Annie Olson & Parents
Bill, Margaret, Melanie & Lauren Olson
Dana, Jeff, Jason, Lisa Ovadia
Mike & Greg Padgett
The Palitz Family
Thatcher Palmer & Elaine & George Shelby
Susan, Bruce & Marissa Paltenghi
The Jim Pappageorge Family
The Paradis Family
Ray, Susie, John & Lauren Parker
The Paulsen Family
The Stephan Peers Family
The Pegnim Family
Mr. & Mrs. Caesar Perales & Family
Larry, Connie & Luke Peterson
Robin Phillips & Family
Steven & Karen Phillips
The Pinkham Family
Tom, Sally, Katie & Johnny Pitts
The Plant Family
Vlad, Jana, Jan & Martin Pochop
The Poetzsch Family
The Pohl Family
Stan, Dawn, Eli & Briel Pomerantz
David & Elisabeth Potts
Kathleen, Alexander, Ryan, Kellen & Katherine Poulos

The Powers Family
The Pricco Family
Edward, Carole, Jeff & Eric Price
Ned, Marcia, Michael &
  Stefanie Putnam
Michael & Sheia Rasooly
Lori & Meghan Ratto
Mike & Linda Ream & Children
Michael & Natalie Reeder
Jeffrey & Ana Resnik
The Revelli Family
The Ricksen Family
Dr. Lawrence, Toby, Shoshana &
  Daniella Risman
The Ritchie Family
Stacey & Kelly Robbins
The Rockwells
The Rondeau-Nicoli Family
Bill, Beverly, Sara & Katie Rose
Tom & Carolyn Rowland & Family
Svend, Charlotta, Katie, Steffen &
  Andreas Ryge
Shari, Dave, Kim & Michael Safianoff
Jason & Mira Salameh
Schareef & Kanaan Sarakbi
Kreyne, Laura, Russ & Kirk Sato
Art & Susan Savage
Diane, Al & Daniel Scali
John & Susan Schlicher
John, Timmy, Molly, Alex &
  Tina Schmid

Doug, Karen, Emma & Katie Schneider
Lillian & Sidney Schneider
Bill, Patsy, Jeffrey & Kevin Schrupp
Bobk, Karin, Lindsey, Lauren &
  Joshua Schubert
The Schwartz Family
The Schwertscharf Family
Sumner, Cindy, Scott, Matthew &
  Alexandra Seibert
Jon, Lee & Carrie Shaffer
Ben & Sandy Shaw
The Sheehan Family
JoAnn, Andy, Andrew, Jonathan &
  Alex Shogan
John, Michele, Robin & John Siegfried
The Signorella Family
Cheri, Glenn, Alaynn, Edlyn &
  Galen Smith
Mychelle, Kevin, Susie & Courtney Smith
Jim & Sue Somers & Family
Tam & Mike Soon
Frank, Bonnie, Andrew & Alyson Sorba
The Souza Family
The Spease Family
The Spence Family
Richard, Linda & Erika Staaf
Christopher Stark & Family
Rick, Caren, Lindsay & Courtney Steffens
Daniel, Dick & Judy Stern
Steve, Barbara, Tova & Jordana
Chris, Barbara, Matt, Mark &
  Meghan Stevens

The Straus Family
Mark, Kim, Kate, Jenna & Blair Stubbe
The Sturman Family
Dave, Judy, Lori, Scott & Adam Sutch
Bob, Bonnie, Kristi & Andrew Symon
Hugh, Sharon, Loren & Samantha Tama
The Tamas Family with appetites
The Tammen Family
The Tarapores
Bob, Rose, Chrissy & Robin Taylor
Bob, Cathy, Carey, Chris &
    Dana Terry
Mr. & Mrs. Jon Thallaug
Cody & Adam Thomas' Family
Ramsay, Janet, Mary, Annie &
    Joey Thomas
Virginia Thomsen
The Tiernan Family
The Tiras Family
The Tom Family
Jim, Diane, Jimmy & Danny Tomkins
Clyde, Marilyn & Brian
    Townsend-Elmore
The Tses
George & Alice Turner
Jerilou, Paul & Becky Twohey
Tiffany Ulbrich
The Tim Valentines
Janet Van Etten
Barney, Pat, Clint & Vicki Van Horn
Erin & J.P. Viera
The Villata Family

The Wagner Family
Jim, Bonnie, Sarah & Katie Walsh
Kathleen, Greg, Jim & Jane Walsh
Mitch, Ann & Michael Ward
The William W. Ward III Family
Sandy, Scott & Tib Warner
Chris, Larry & Jean Watson
Ed, Denise, Kelley & Kristin Webster
Kate Webster & Family
The Wellman Family
Michael, Peggy, Heather &
    Lauren White
Holly Wieber & Patrick, Lorey &
    Charles White,
Richard & Nancy White
Karen Nakkerud & Don, Lisa &
    Brian Whiteside
The Wihera Family
The Wille Family
Jesse, Marie & Andrea Williams
Jerry, Kathy, Elizabeth & Erika Wilson
Jim & Christy Wilson & Family
Kristen, Erin, Alison, Gale &
    Bill Wilson
The Wondolowski Family
Norman & Maureen Wong
Joe, Roxie, Adam & Molly Wood
Grant & Scott Woods
Bill, Irma & Asia Wright
Jeff, Rebecca, Kirsten & Chris Wright
The Wullschlegers
The Zuehlke/Mara Family

Notes

Notes

Notes

Notes